shame-informed therapy

Treatment Strategies to Overcome
Core Shame and Reconstruct the Authentic Self

Patti Ashley, PhD, LPC

Shame-Informed Therapy © copyright 2020 by Patti Ashley

Published by:
PESI Publishing & Media
PESI, Inc.
3839 White Ave.
Eau Claire, WI 54703

Cover Design: Amy Rubenzer
Editing By: Jenessa Jackson, PhD
Layout: Amy Rubenzer & Bookmasters

Printed in the United States of America
ISBN: 9781683732815
All rights reserved.

PESI
Publishing
& Media
pesipublishing.com

Dedication

Dedicated to *Dr. Katharine Kersey*, my teacher, mentor, and friend. Working and studying with her in the 1990s shined a light into my heart and taught me how to know that I am enough. My life is now dedicated to continuing her legacy of making the world a better place and helping others let their light shine.

About the Author

Patti Ashley, PhD, licensed professional counselor, has integrated 40 years of experience in special education, child development, and psychology into her wholehearted work as a psychotherapist, author, international speaker, and authenticity architect coach. She brings unique insights into the identification and treatment of shame, trauma, grief, and dysfunctional family patterns.

Dr. Ashley owns and operates *Authenticity Architects* in Boulder, Colorado. Her inimitable *Authenticity Architecture* model facilitates long-term changes in the brain and nervous system, helping clients break through unconscious barriers and rediscover a sense of self-love, belonging, and connection. As a licensed professional counselor since 2000, Dr. Ashley has counseled a myriad of individuals, couples, families and groups in mental health agencies, psychiatric hospitals, and private practice settings. She also has many years of experience developing continuing education courses for physicians, hospital wellness programs, universities, and other organizations.

Patti holds a Doctor of Philosophy Degree in psychology from the Union Institute and University, a Master of Education Degree in early childhood from Old Dominion University, and a Bachelor of Science Degree in special education from James Madison University. She is the author of *Living in the Shadow of the Too-Good Mother Archetype* (2014), *Letters to Freedom* (2019), and *Shame-Informed Therapy: Treatment Strategies to Overcome Core Shame and Reconstruct the Authentic Self* (2020). For more information, please visit www.pattiashley.com.

Table of Contents

Part I: Definitions, Research, and Implications for Shame-Informed Therapy

Part II: The Art and Architecture of Reconstructing the Authentic Self

Acknowledgments

Writing a book is no easy task. Hours of commitment and dedication to the process leave less time for friends and family. So I want to start off by thanking my friends and family for being patient with me every time I had to say, "I can't this weekend, I'm working on my book." And I want to extend an extra special thank-you to the ones who reached out and said, "How's it going?"

I am forever grateful to my four grown children for being my biggest teachers. Without them, I wouldn't have learned how to love so deeply and reach so far to learn what little people need to grow up to be awesome humans. Thank you!

And thank you to my many teachers along the way. Both the ones I have met in person and the ones I know only from their books. I am grateful for the inspiration that these luminaries have passed on to me through their teaching and gifts. Katharine Kersey, T. Berry Brazelton, Mary Elizabeth Marlow, Pat McNeal, Jeremy Taylor, Billie Ortiz, Donna Remmert, Laura Deal, Barbara Kersey, Kelly Sullivan Walden, Sister Claire, Pat Ogden, Joan Borysenko, Harville Hendrix, Helen Hunt, DeAnn Davies, Nicholas Kasovec, M. Willson Williams, Paul Solari, Andrew Bunin, David Delaney, Laurence Freedom, Marcy Cooper, and Joan Schaublin are just a few I have had the pleasure of meeting in person. However, there are many others I have not met whom I've referenced throughout this book, such as Brené Brown, Gershen Kaufman, Allan Schore, Stephen Porges, Bessel van der Kolk, Peter Levine, Marianne Williamson, Carolyn Myss, and many other incredible teachers. Thank you!

I also am grateful for the chance to present workshops on shame in clinical practice for PESI and, furthermore, to now be publishing this book that is so near and dear to my heart with their publishing division. Thank you Karsyn Morse for your willingness to publish it, the inspiration to help me with revisions, and the patience to wait for my edits. And thank you Jenessa Jackson for your meticulous edits and keen eye while putting the book together in a seamlessly flowing fashion.

And anyone I may have forgotten to mention, please know you are deeply held in my heart. Thank you!

All in all, it's been a good ride, and my gratitude extends to the moon and back!

Introduction

"Like a wound made from the inside by an unseen hand, shame disrupts the natural functioning of the self. If we are to understand and eventually heal what ails the self, then we must begin with shame."

—Dr. Gershen Kaufman

Shame-Informed Therapy

Building and sustaining positive therapeutic relationships is hard work. Clinicians sometimes report feeling stuck and unsure of the reasons clinical strategies aren't working. Identifying and looking at treatment through the lens of shame provides therapists some insight into a missing link in effective treatment (Lewis, 1971).

Current shame research has revealed a common experience of "not enoughness" in our Western culture (Brown, 2007). In particular, present-day society is characterized by a constant striving to attain perfection and live up to societal expectations. Clients frequently say things such as, "I'll never get it right," "I never feel good enough," and "I don't know what's wrong with me, everyone else seems to be able to manage their life." This striving to be good enough is a clear indicator of a deeper, unconscious manifestation of core shame. This shame-based fear of being exposed as flawed can create an overexaggerated need to be perfect and free of mistakes.

Perfectionism is "an overwhelming driving tension to get everything right, to appear sinless and flawless, so as to avoid the critical scrutiny of others and not be exposed as weak, vulnerable, a sham, or fraudulent" (Yard, 2014, p. 45). Perfectionism differs from striving to do the best one can and taking steps toward self-improvement because it is self-destructive and impossible to attain. Shame is born out of perfectionism because no one is perfect (Brown, 2010a).

The experience of not enoughness shows up clearly in perfectionism, but you can also see it in clients who isolate, underachieve, blame others, or put on a facade in an attempt to cover up core shame. Yet this not enoughness can easily remain undetected by clinicians. **Core shame is like an infectious disease that goes untreated because its symptoms are difficult to diagnose.** Core shame is the missing element lurking beneath many common diagnoses and often isn't easy to recognize.

The five common components of core shame include low self-esteem, humiliation, problems with self-continuity, isolation or not fitting in, and the feeling of being watched by others (Akhtar, 2009). Shame is different from guilt in that shame is deeply embodied as a sense of self, while guilt happens during a particular experience of hurting someone or doing something that feels disrespectful or inappropriate. Shame is more silent and difficult to access (Lewis, 1988).

Figure 1. Shame Hub

Core shame is like the hub of a wheel (Figure 1) because it can hide under numerous other behaviors or diagnoses. It might manifest as lying, perfectionism, denial, minimization, grandiosity, narcissistic self-inflation, rationalization, rage, avoidance, hopelessness, or projection (Yard, 2014). Shame-informed therapy is continuously searching for hidden core shame and the defenses against it. It is only when the clinician begins to see the client through the fine-tuned lens of shame that it becomes more evident how most of these symptoms could represent a defense against shame.

Core shame is so painful and contagious that the witness to shame often looks the other way. Therapists are no exception (Lewis, 1988). The origin of the word *shame* means "to cover." A client's unconscious shame can be so powerful that the therapist can get caught up in the projections and thus feel inadequate to the task. It is important for shame-informed therapists to look at their own unconscious experiences of shame-proneness in order to better tolerate and co-regulate with clients (DeYoung, 2015).

Early shame researcher Helen Lewis called shame the "sleeper" emotion because it is not easily recognized, and she proposed that when therapists fail to recognize core shame as a critical aspect of treatment, problems worsen (Lewis, 1971). When the therapist doesn't have fine-tuned empathic listening skills, which are needed to identify core shame, clinical interventions can easily trigger more shame, spiraling the client into other affective experiences such as embarrassment, guilt, or obsessive worry (Lewis, 1988).

In contrast, when clinicians understand how shame influences the therapeutic relationship, treatment is more effective, as clinicians can then build more sustainable strategies that improve treatment outcomes. Creating authentic relationships with clients and trusting the individualized process allows clinicians to step more fully into unconditional positive regard (Rogers, 1961). This process allows the client to feel *good enough* as the therapist sees into and feels the client's experience with empathy, which is the antidote to shame (DeYoung, 2015).

Core shame erodes the ability to recognize what Donald Winnicott (1986) labeled the true self, or the essence of what one has been born to be. Instead, a false self emerges, and in an attempt to feel lovable, clients create stories about themselves based on what others have suggested they become, or they develop faulty coping mechanisms. That is, the false self develops based on what others want. It over-conforms and only loves conditionally. It hides, covers, or denies feelings (Whitfield, 1987).

Shame-informed therapy offers tools that help clients excavate their true self as they begin to recognize the defenses against core shame they have developed over time. This involves integrating the right- and left-brain functions, as well as regulating the autonomic nervous system in order to reconstruct a more authentic self.

Through this lens of reconstructing the authentic self, this workbook seeks to provide a framework for treating core shame in clinical practice. It provides some guidelines that help clinicians excavate the origins of shame and better identify the nonverbal, unspoken, and unseen aspects in their clinical work. It is intended for mental health professionals who work with clients struggling with anxiety, depression, mood disorders, relationship difficulties, or chronic low self-esteem. However, the exercises in this book can be helpful in other circumstances as well, as core shame is a universal human experience.

What Is in This Book

The workbook is divided into two parts. **Part 1** helps clinicians look more closely at the therapeutic process from the very fine lens of shame-informed therapy, providing an overview of early shame research and current neurobiological findings illustrating how core shame gets wired into the brain and nervous system. It also discusses the stages of building and maintaining a therapeutic relationship characterized by empathy and safety.

Part 2 provides a multimodal approach for working with right- and left-brain co-regulation and the autonomic nervous system in therapy. This approach integrates Stephen Porges's (2009) four therapeutic R's—(1) **R**ecognizing the autonomic state the client is in, (2) **R**especting the adaptive survival response, (3) Co-**R**egulating with the client into a state of safety, and (4) **R**e-storying—with other bottom-up and top-down psychotherapy approaches, creative arts, metaphor, and dreamwork to provide clinicians a framework for working with core shame.

Even though working with core shame is often a nonlinear process, **Part 2** attempts to present an outline of some therapeutic interventions that integrate the brain's right and left hemispheres and that calm the nervous system. These tools and techniques are intended to rewire neural pathways in the right brain by providing clients with experiences that bring emotional safety, joy, playfulness, and comfort. This process is likened to art and architecture: The art of the right brain lends for creativity and flow, while the architecture of the left brain helps rewire the neural pathways necessary to reconstruct a story of safety in the body.

Throughout this workbook, the acronym SELF is used to describe a **S**afe **E**xperience of **L**iving **F**reely, which is the ultimate goal of treating shame. Consistent with this goal, clinicians will find exercises, worksheets, handouts, and meditations that can be useful in helping clients navigate the process of re-storying their core shame narrative into one of an authentic SELF. Some of the exercises ask clients to journal about their experiences as a way to acknowledge and express feelings and dig up core shame. For clients who are open to writing, these journal assignments can be a valuable supplement to the exercises in this book. These clients might benefit from bringing a notebook to session so they can take down notes and jot down homework assignments.

For clients who don't like writing, I suggest other somatic and creative forms of expression. For example, they can repeat affirmations that they learned in the session throughout the week while taking a shower or walking the dog. As you build the relationship across time, listen for clues to other creative or somatic outlets.

Finally, in the sections called **Sample Re-Story**, I provide examples illustrating segments of re-storying. Ultimately, shame-informed therapy seeks to help clients rewrite a new narrative of authentic safety and connection that overrides the shame and gives them the ability to find self-compassion and acceptance. The goal is to return shame to its origin, helping the client excavate and develop a more congruent SELF.

part I

definitions, research, and implications for shame-informed therapy

*"Children come into the world like a packet of seeds with no cover on the front.
It is our job, very much like a gardener's, to provide the adequate water, air, light,
and nutrition that the seed needs to grow to its fullest potential. It is not our job
to raise a rose into a carnation or a carnation into a rose."*

—Dr. Katharine Kersey

1

What Is Core Shame?

"Shame isn't a quiet grey cloud, shame is a drowning man who claws his way on top of you, scratching and tearing your skin, pushing you under the surface."

—Kirsty Eagar

The Difference Between Shame and Core Shame

Shame is a primary emotion that functions as a moral compass in repairing and maintaining relationships. When we feel remorseful for hurting another person or for doing something that violates our sense of integrity, shame can lead us to make amends and allow us to learn how not to repeat the same mistake again. It is a mechanism of social control that deters us from hurting ourselves or others, and it underlies the formation of conscience (Rothschild, 2000).

Although shame is an adaptive emotion that prevents people from acting out of pure self-interest, shame can become maladaptive when there are repeated breaches in trust and safety in interpersonal relationships over time. For example, repeated loss of connection with a primary caregiver during early childhood (e.g., due to abuse or neglect) can negatively impact brain development and lead to the internalization of what is known as *core shame*.

When people think of shame, they often think of events or situations that are clearly associated with feelings of humiliation, guilt, or remorse, such as sexual abuse or relapse in addiction. Even though these circumstances are certainly characterized by shame, core shame is a deeper underlying sense of being unworthy of love and belonging that may or may not have an external situation in view (Brown, 2010a).

Shame Starts with Attachment

What we have learned from attachment theory is that as the nonverbal right brain develops, it is crucial for caregivers to attune to an infant's needs and consistently meet these needs by creating a safe and secure space from which infants can develop, which Winnicott (1986) has referred to as a "holding environment." In optimal right-brain development, the neural networks produce an internal feeling of safety and love from which children are able to develop a sense of trust and connection. These early caregiver relationships thus play a large role in shaping the emotional and social connections one will experience throughout life.

More recently, brain imaging studies have confirmed what early attachment theorists such as Mary Ainsworth and John Bowlby proposed. For example, research by Allan Schore on affect regulation theory has confirmed that "reciprocal right-lateralized visual-facial, auditory-prosodic, and tactile-gestural nonverbal communication between the infant and primary caregiver" (2014, p. 1049) are crucial for optimal brain development. These nonverbal sensory communications between the child and primary caregiver contribute greatly to the expansion of the young child's right-brain regulatory systems, which we now know is mostly formed by three years of age.

However, if a child repeatedly does not have what Donald Winnicott called "good enough" experiences of unconditional love and acceptance, then the compass for trust and connection becomes impaired. This can lead to prolonged shame states that impact the development of neural networks related to emotion regulation and safety in the social brain (Schore, 2019). In particular, the neural networks associated with distrust become activated, whereas those associated with internal feelings of safety and trust become weaker and are then pruned off, very much like how a gardener prunes a bush or a tree. This leads to a lowered capacity for internal feelings of SELF.

As a child's language begins to develop, the left brain then constructs a narrative, or story, of what is happening in the nonverbal right brain, attempting to integrate prosodic and interpersonal elements that were set up early on. This story forms a sense of self, weaving together the child's internal and external experiences. For example, if a child is told that they will never amount to anything, then they may develop a story that they are worthless or a disappointment. In turn, they may repeatedly fail at tasks set before them or, conversely, overachieve in an attempt to never make a mistake. Similarly, if a client grows up in a household in which their feelings are never acknowledged, or they are explicitly shamed for showing emotion, then they may develop the narrative that expressing their feelings is bad. Shame eventually becomes internalized within their personality, and the narrative shifts from "I did something bad" to "I am bad" (Brown, 2007).

Figure 2 illustrates a few of the core shame personas, which include: "I'm bad," "I'm a fraud," "I'm flawed," "I'm never good enough," "I'm a failure," "I'm not lovable," and "I'm not worthy of love," to name a few. There are many other ways the core shame identity can manifest in addition to those listed here.

Big and Little Ruptured Interpersonal Bridges

The bond between two individuals forms an interpersonal bridge between them, and when there are repeated ruptures in these interpersonal bridges—as in the case of a "not good enough" attachment environment—a core shame identity develops in which there is an overarching fear of being exposed as fundamentally deficient and tragically flawed (Kaufman, 1974). This results in a chronic sense of unworthiness, unlovability, and disconnection. The ability to have empathy for the self is lost in an environment that isn't empathetic.

When the primary caregiver repeatedly lacks attunement and there is repeated, unrepaired disconnection between the caregiver and child, this creates a disintegration in self-awareness. This disintegration makes it difficult for clients to access a coherent self. The disintegrated

Figure 2. Core Shame Identity

self may manifest in therapy as depression, anxiety, depletion, or fragmentation (DeYoung, 2015). At times, it may even be difficult for clients to think or speak clearly.

Although the experiences of ruptured interpersonal bridges start with attachment, these ruptures continue further as children move out into the world and form other relationships. Teachers, friends, coworkers, employers, and even therapists and physicians can cause ruptures in interpersonal bridges. Trauma, abuse, neglect, bullying, and repeated failures can proliferate shame as individuals continue into adulthood. Any type of trauma in one's lifetime can recreate the same shame-inducing qualities learned from the originally ruptured interpersonal bridges (Kaufman, 1992).

The right-brain impairment that results from trauma often goes hand in hand with shame, and both involve similar neurobiological processes. In the case of trauma, we tend to classify certain events as big "T" traumas (such as natural disasters, sexual assault, or situations that involve threatened or actual injury) and other events as little "t" traumas (such as divorce, job loss, and emotional abuse). Similarly, we can also classify shame in degree by considering the severity of the ruptures in interpersonal bridges. Larger shame-inducing events, such as abuse and neglect, might be considered big bridge ruptures, whereas smaller shame-inducing events, such as outdated shamed-based parenting practices, might be considered little bridge ruptures. Nonetheless, the core identity of shame takes hold regardless of the degree of ruptures, and we should treat it as such.

Sometimes, clients minimize their experience of shame by comparing it to larger and more easily identified experiences. For example, a client who was teased and taunted for being overweight as a child might think his shame is "not a big deal" because his friend was sexually abused as a child. Clinicians need to treat all degrees of shame, both the big and little ruptured bridges, with the same amount of empathy and compassion because the sensory messages stored in implicit memories all require unconditional positive regard, no matter how big or small.

Regardless of whether shame results from a little or big bridge rupture, we store early experiences of core shame in the implicit memory system, which is unconscious, emotional, sensory, body-oriented, automatic, and nonverbal. This is in contrast to explicit memories, which are conscious, cognitive, verbal, linear, and factual. As a result, shame can be difficult to diagnosis and treat in practice because clients may not have any explicit memories of the specific events that lead to the ruptures in the interpersonal bridges, especially in the first three years of their life when the nonverbal right brain is primarily developing. Instead, shame lurks underground in the nonverbal, unconscious mind.

Shame-informed therapy involves bringing the unconscious to consciousness by excavating the implicit memories of shame. The emotions and sensations in the body memory can then give the client and clinician further clues to the earlier ruptures in interpersonal bridges. From there, the clinician begins to make connections related to the development of core shame based on the recognition of the social-emotional developmental need that may have been unmet at the time.

The Evolution of Social-Emotional Development

Prior to the mid-twentieth century, knowledge of social-emotional development was lacking. Furthermore, the average human life span was shorter, and basic survival needs often took precedent over social-emotional ones. Parents were taught how to raise children based on information taken from biblical texts and sources that encouraged adults to be the "masters," and children were taught to be subservient to them. For example, eighteenth century child-rearing textbooks taught parents that *all* feelings were bad, and children were consequently punished for expressing them (Miller, 1983). Parents were taught that they should discourage high self-esteem, not respond to a child's needs, be cold and severe to better prepare children for life, not respect children, not be tender or doting with children, and "break the will" of the child before he or she was old enough to remember (Miller, 1983).

Current child development research has indicated this is far from what children need for optimal brain development. We now know that healthy attachment is key to social-emotional development and that children observe and download a caregiver's beliefs and behaviors as their own. Once these beliefs and behaviors are imprinted into a child's implicit memory, typically by the age of seven, they become biologically hardwired for a lifetime—unless a conscious effort is made to excavate and reprogram them (Lipton, 2005).

Unfortunately, many of the outdated shame-based parenting practices are still in use today and can cause significant ruptures in interpersonal relationship bridges, contributing to the development of a core shame identity. Even though these parenting techniques may not appear to be explicit forms of abuse and may still fall under the category of seemingly appropriate "discipline," they are fundamentally shame-based in nature and proliferate internal feelings of emotion dysregulation and potentially core shame.

For example, I was grocery shopping the other day and noticed a woman strolling the aisles with a five-year-old sitting in the front of her shopping cart. I observed the woman smile and jokingly say to the child, "I don't know how your mother puts up with you." When I looked at the child's face, there was no smile there. Instead, I saw a very sad frown as the child slouched over in the shopping cart, looking quite withdrawn. Although the woman was not consciously trying to impose shame on the child, as evidenced by her smile and joking manner, the comment *was* quite shaming nonetheless. She gave the child a message that she was unlovable. This type of teasing happens often to children. I see it all the time. To me, it represents the unconscious repetition of old parenting beliefs, such as "children should be seen and not heard," and the misunderstood idea that children think like adults.

However, according to Piaget's theory of cognitive development (1969), children under the age of seven can't distinguish fantasy from reality. Therefore, the messages that a parent or caregiver gives to a child seem real, and the child equates those messages as truth. That is what happened in the interaction I witnessed in the grocery store: The child did not interpret the woman's message as funny, even though that is how the woman intended it, and instead interpreted it as shaming.

When children are talked out of their feelings with all-too-familiar comments—such as "Stop crying before I give you something to cry about" or "You should be ashamed of yourself"—they develop the belief that not only are their feelings bad, but they too are bad. As adults, they tend to dismiss their feelings and are often unable to even access them anymore. Understanding these subtleties of cognitive development can help us better understand how important words are in the development of core shame.

In addition, recent studies on transgenerational trauma have indicated that ancestral trauma is passed down in our DNA across generations (Youssef et al., 2018). This might explain part of the reason why parents repeat patterns that they learned growing up even though they know better parenting practices: We are clearly living in the shadow of old parenting beliefs. Learning new parenting practices requires excavating old wounds, being very conscious of patterns that need to change, and doing the inner work required to make those shifts. Whether or not clients are parents of young children, the work of shame-informed therapy addresses the repair from past generational trauma in order to reconstruct a more congruent, authentic self.

Why Self-Compassion Is So Hard to Access

Self-compassion has three main qualities: (1) self-kindness (being kind to ourselves when we are suffering), (2) a sense of connection to humanity (recognizing that everyone is imperfect and that everyone suffers), and (3) mindfulness (nonjudgmentally accepting our experiences, even those that are painful) (Neff, 2003). However, self-compassion is not easily accessed in shame. **Most clients who harbor underlying shame report that they do not know how to love themselves.** For them, self-compassion feels like an impossible task because it makes them feel too vulnerable and subject to other's judgment (Campion & Glover, 2017).

Additionally, because the influence of outdated child-rearing practices still permeates Western culture, many individuals have also internalized the belief that they shouldn't honor their feelings or think too highly of themselves (Miller, 1983).

Trying to talk clients out of the belief that they are unlovable is virtually impossible because the memory of being not good enough lives in the implicit sensory memory. Therefore, working with core shame requires activating right-brain memories with the understanding that it takes time to adequately change unconscious beliefs. Psychoeducational opportunities are excellent ways to help clients understand why it feels impossible to access self-compassion. When we educate our clients, we begin to demystify the shame. As clients begin to understand the impact of trauma and stress on development, including how the feeling of being not good enough has become encoded in the body and subconscious mind, they begin to realize that the circumstances that led to their current struggles were outside of their control and that perhaps they aren't so flawed after all.

It is important to note that some clients may believe they have escaped the effects of early shaming conditions. High-functioning clients may even claim they do not experience any shame at all. **However, clinicians should still pay close attention to underlying indicators of shame, such as anxiety, perfectionism, grandiosity, or minimization.** These clients may not be able to tolerate or recognize their own shame. For them, it is too shaming and elusive. They may mention that they have low self-esteem but that they don't see that as shame. The difference in the two is that self-esteem lives in thought patterns, and shame lives in emotional body memories.

Exercises

To gather information about a client's core shame history, clinicians can use the following three worksheets as a guide. The **It Wasn't Your Fault** worksheet helps clients recognize how their past circumstances have shaped the development of their sense of self. **The "Not-Enough" Messages Learned as a Child** worksheet helps clients identify the negative messages they received in childhood that may have contributed to unconscious shame-based beliefs. The **Person, Place, or Thing** worksheet is a clear guide to the developmental milestones related to how core shame may get set up in the body based on life events. You can use these worksheets as a reference point for clinical inquiries or offer them to clients directly if they are not too triggering to complete on their own.

It Wasn't Your Fault

You develop a sense of who you are from your experiences with others. Your earliest understanding about relationships may have been impaired owing to circumstances beyond your control. For example, your parents may have ignored or downplayed your proudest accomplishments, or they may have told you that you would never amount to anything. As a child, you may have internalized these experiences and thought you caused them.

This worksheet helps you identify some of the things that happened so you can develop more self-compassion and self-acceptance. Take your time answering the questions. There are no right or wrong answers. Simply note what comes to mind. If any question feels too uncomfortable, skip it and move on to the next one, or stop the exercise and find a calming activity or mindful meditation to relax for a while before continuing later.

My first memory as a child is:

_____

_____

_____

_____

My parents were:

_____

_____

_____

_____

What I learned about love as a child is:

_____

_____

_____

_____

I was disciplined through:

_____

_____

_____

_____

Communication in my family was challenging because:

_____

_____

_____

_____

What I learned about myself as a child was:

_____

_____

_____

_____

My favorite play as a child was:

_____

_____

_____

_____

The "Not-Enough" Messages Learned as a Child

Many of us were raised in families where the implicit or explicit message of "you are not good enough" was a common thread in the household. These messages about not enoughness may have had to do with your academic performance, your athletic achievements, your appearance, or your overall worth as a human being. The following list contains some "not-enough" messages you may have heard growing up. Check the ones you remember hearing as a child. Who did you hear the message from? How old were you? Add any other messages that come to mind. If you'd like, write more about these memories and feelings in your journal.

"Not-Enough" Message	The Person Telling Me This Was:	My Age Was:
❑ You'll never amount to anything.		
❑ You should be ashamed of yourself.		
❑ Stop crying before I give you something to cry about.		
❑ Don't be angry.		
❑ Get over yourself and be happy.		
❑ Stop that attitude.		
❑ You need to respect me.		
❑ Give your grandmother (or another person) a kiss.		

"Not-Enough" Message	The Person Telling Me This Was:	My Age Was:
❑ Children should be seen and not heard.		
❑ Do it because I said so.		
❑ You are getting too big for your britches.		
❑ You look ugly.		
❑ You are fat.		
❑ Why can't you be more like your brother (or sister)?		
❑ You are so selfish.		
❑ You should be grateful for what you have.		
❑ Don't be such a crybaby.		
❑ You'll go blind if you masturbate.		
❑ Aren't you "little miss (or mister) know-it-all"?		
❑ Who do you think you are?		
❑ Act your age and not your shoe size.		
❑ You're an idiot.		

"Not-Enough" Message	The Person Telling Me This Was:	My Age Was:
❑ You are so clumsy.		
❑ You're a lazy bum.		
❑ You look like a whore.		
❑ I trust you about as far as I can throw you.		
❑ You'll be okay; you are a dumb blonde.		
❑ What do you know? Nothing, that's what.		
❑ You're crazy.		
❑ Grow up.		
❑ You're the luckiest kid alive, so how can you complain?		
❑ Suck it up.		
❑ How come you don't have a boyfriend (or girlfriend) yet?		
❑ Your hair is a mess, let me fix it.		
❑ Write your own.		
❑ Write your own.		

Person, Place, or Thing

As a result of research in the past century, we now know that children think very differently from adults. Before then, children were thought of as small adults and treated in ways that did not adequately meet their developmental needs. The work of Erik Erikson in particular helped us better understand development across the life span, as he created a model outlining the psychosocial stages of development from birth to death. These developmental stages include trust versus mistrust, autonomy versus shame, initiative versus guilt, industry versus inferiority, identity versus role confusion, intimacy versus isolation, generativity versus stagnation, and integrity versus despair.

Why is this important? You might have memories of certain people, places, or things at various times in your life that correspond with these developmental stages. For instance, the second stage, autonomy versus shame, is all about learning to be a self that is separate from your caregivers. If you were told no often or punished for being curious during this stage, then it could have influenced your ability to feel confident and autonomous.

Use this worksheet or your journal to write down your thoughts and feelings about memories that occurred at each of these stages of development. Only fill in the stages of development through which you have already advanced. Take your time—one stage and memory at a time!

Trust Versus Mistrust (0–1.5 years)

An infant needs a stable and consistent primary caregiver in order to feel safe. If this occurs, then a sense of *trust* develops. But if care is inconsistent or unstable, then a sense of *mistrust* develops.

Hope is the optimal outcome of this stage.

I remember (or had someone tell me about) this person, place, or thing and these feelings during this time in my life:

_____

_____

_____

_____

_____

_____

_____

Autonomy Versus Shame (1.5–3 years)

Toddlers in this stage are developing a sense of independence and *autonomy*. If toddlers are encouraged and supported in demonstrating independence, then they will feel confident and secure. But if they are frequently criticized or overly controlled, then a sense of *shame* or doubt may develop.

Will is the optimal outcome of this stage.

I remember (or had someone tell me about) this person, place, or thing and these feelings during this time in my life:

_____

_____

_____

_____

_____

_____

_____

_____

_____

_____

Initiative Versus Guilt (3-5 years)

The preschooler explores their interpersonal skills through play and interacting with others. When they are presented with adequate opportunities for interaction and play, then a sense of *initiative* and confidence in making decisions develops. If this initiative is suppressed, then they can develop a sense of *guilt*, or the feeling of being a nuisance, which results in a lack of initiative.

Purpose is the optimal outcome of this stage.

I remember (or had someone tell me about) this person, place, or thing and these feelings during this time in my life:

_____

_____

_____

_____

_____

_____

_____

_____

_____

_____

_____

Industry Versus Inferiority (5–12 years)

In the early school years, children are learning how to read, write, do math problems, and accomplish other academic tasks on their own. Teachers and peers play a large role in the development of self-esteem. If we encourage children to try out these new skills, then they develop a feeling of *industry*, competence, and confidence in achieving their goals. If we do not encourage them, then they may doubt themselves and have difficulty excelling, resulting in a sense of *inferiority*.

Competence is the optimal outcome of this stage.

I remember this person, place, or thing and these feelings during this time in my life:

_____

_____

_____

_____

_____

_____

_____

_____

_____

_____

Ego Identity Versus Role Confusion (12–18 years)

Teenagers are searching for sexual and occupational identities as they begin to identify their beliefs, values, and goals. A sense of *identity* is formed based on those explorations. Failure to answer some of those questions might create a sense of *role confusion*.

Fidelity is the optimal outcome of this stage.

I remember this person, place, or thing and these feelings during this time in my life:

_____

_____

_____

_____

_____

_____

_____

_____

_____

_____

_____

Intimacy Versus Isolation (18–40 years)

Commitments outside of the family begin to occur after high school and into early adulthood. If individuals are able to develop satisfying and loving relationships, then this can provide them with a sense of *intimacy*, commitment, and safety within relationships. However, if they are unable to form intimate relationships, then *isolation* and loneliness may develop.

Love is the optimal outcome of this stage.

I remember this person, place, or thing and these feelings during this time in my life:

_____

_____

_____

_____

_____

_____

_____

_____

_____

_____

_____

_____

Generativity Versus Stagnation (40-65 years)

In the later years of adulthood, individuals are focused on creating things that will benefit others and that will persist even after they leave this earth, which results in *generativity* or a glimpse of "the bigger picture." However, if they are unable to find ways to contribute, then a feeling of *stagnation* and disconnection may result.

Care is the optimal outcome of this stage.

I remember this person, place, or thing and these feelings during this time in my life:

_____

_____

_____

_____

_____

_____

_____

_____

_____

_____

_____

_____

Ego Integrity Versus Despair (65+)

During this stage, older adults slow down, explore life, and possibly retire from their careers. If individuals feel they have led a meaningful life, then a sense of *integrity* develops. However, if they believe their lives have been a waste or that they haven't accomplished what they set out to do, then they may experience *despair*, depression, and hopelessness.

Wisdom is the optimal outcome of this stage.

I remember this person, place, or thing and these feelings during this time in my life:

_____

_____

_____

_____

_____

_____

_____

_____

_____

_____

Source: Adapted from *Identity: Youth and Crisis* by E. H. Erikson, W. W. Norton, 1968.

2

The Neurobiology of Shame

"There is a wisdom of the head, and [...] there is a wisdom of the heart."
—Charles Dickens

The Vagus Nerve (aka The Wanderer)

The experience of shame is associated with changes in autonomic nervous system functioning that are best understood through the lens of Stephen Porges's polyvagal theory, which is similarly relevant to working with both trauma and shame. In particular, the polyvagal theory offers us an understanding of the role of the vagus nerve in autonomic nervous system regulation. The vagus nerve is the largest of the twelve cranial nerves and is sometimes referred to as the "wanderer," as it extends from the brainstem into the chest and abdomen (Figure 3). It influences the throat, lungs, heart, digestion, and elimination (Rosenberg, 2017). Eighty percent of the vagus nerve sends information from the viscera to the brain, meaning that it provides sensory input from our visceral organs to our brain about how our body is feeling. These messages convey information to the nervous system about our sense of safety, or lack thereof, in our surroundings.

According to Porges's polyvagal theory, the autonomic nervous system comprises a tripartite, phylogenetic hierarchical structure that has evolved over time, expanding our previous two-part understanding that comprised only the sympathetic and parasympathetic nervous systems. In particular, Porges identified three subsystems in the hierarchy: the dorsal vagal complex, the sympathetic nervous system, and the ventral vagal complex. Each subsystem is associated with different states of immobilization, physiological states, emotional responses, visceral reactions, and behavioral responses (Porges, 2017).

The oldest and most primitive branch of the autonomic nervous system is the *dorsal vagal complex*. This is the part of the parasympathetic nervous system that is involved in immobilizing the body or sending it into a "freeze" response when there is a perceived threat from which there is no escape (Dana, 2018). When the dorsal vagal complex is activated, feelings of hopelessness, helplessness, withdrawal, shutdown, and apathy may result (Rosenberg, 2017).

The next system to evolve is the *sympathetic nervous system*. This is the branch of the autonomic nervous system that mobilizes the body to take action by initiating the fight-or-flight

Parasympathetic System

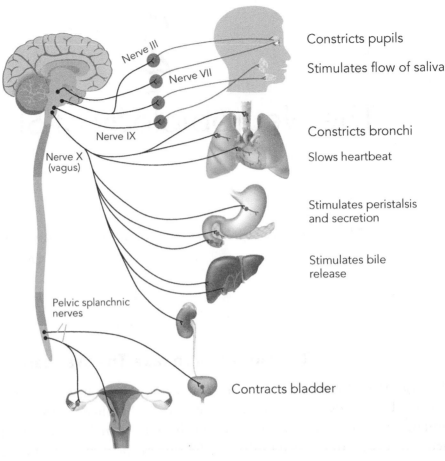

Figure 3. The Vagus Nerve

response. It functions to support movement by increasing cardiac input and propelling extraordinary life-saving efforts when there is the perception of a threat (Porges, 2017). If the nervous system is functioning optimally, it should return to a state of calm and safety after the threat has passed (Rosenberg, 2017).

Finally, the *ventral vagus complex*, also known as the "social engagement system," is the newest structure to develop. It reflects the part of the parasympathetic nervous system that promotes connection and social engagement when there is a feeling of safety. To engage socially we need to feel emotionally *safe*. If the nervous system is functioning well, then we can access openness, positive expectations, and trust in social interactions. In contrast, if the nervous system feels unsafe, then it is harder for us to access rational thought because our energy moves into defensive, instinctual responses (Porges, 2017). Activating the ventral vagus nerve provides the way out of both mobilization (sympathetic nervous system activation) and immobilization (dorsal vagal activation) from fear.

Neuroception

Underlying Porges's polyvagal theory is the concept of *neuroception*, which describes how the autonomic nervous system responds to cues of safety, danger, and life threat. Neuroception is the body's subconscious system for detecting threats and safety in the environment (Porges, 2004). According to the polyvagal theory, our bodies are constantly evaluating the risk in our surroundings, and this process is one that precedes perception and involves detection without awareness. It is for this reason that a kind face or soothing voice can alter how we feel, and how being seen and heard by the people who care about us helps us feel calm and safe (van der Kolk, 2014).

However, when the experience of social connection is interrupted and there is a loss of co-regulation, this results in a neuroception of threat and what Porges (2017) calls "biological rudeness." This involves an experience of misattunement in which neural expectancies regarding social connection are violated. Similar to a trauma response, when a client is triggered in this manner, the left brain takes over. Thoughts of "I'm not enough," "I'm a failure," "I'll never get it right," and "What is wrong with me?" come to the forefront. The prefrontal cortex goes offline, and the amygdala, a primitive part of the brain, goes into overdrive (Levine, 2010).

Accessing safety and regulating emotions creates a sort of cognitive dissonance where the client is unable to utilize higher levels of thinking. Shame takes control of the wheel, so to speak. When this occurs, clients are unable to feel self-compassion or to let go of the notion that they are "not enough." The inner critic works overtime and never takes a break. In turn, clients may engage in a variety of unproductive responses, such as avoiding others, lashing out, turning inward and judging themselves, or a variety of other behaviors, as seen in the shame hub illustrated in the introduction.

Therefore, tapping into the social engagement system is a critical element in treating shame. We are wired for connection and co-regulation in order to maintain a sense of safety (Cozolino, 2010). Positive early experiences that are "good enough" create neural pathways that regulate the nervous system, contributing to the development of emotional resilience. When the ventral vagus complex is firmly grounded, we feel safe, calm, and connected (Dana, 2018). It is for this reason that regulating or co-regulating with the client into a ventral vagal state is a central component of shame-informed therapy. **When clients are in a state of co-regulation, therapists can help them rewrite a new narrative that overrides shame and that gives them the ability to find more self-compassion, which is a process known as re-storying.**

How the Neurobiology of Shame and Trauma Are Similar

When we work with shame in clinical practice, trauma-informed practices are often helpful, as the neurobiology of shame looks very similar to trauma in the body. Explicit trauma often coincides with implicit shame, and both impact the ability to feel emotionally safe and return to a ventral vagal state. The important part to think about when looking at core shame is how it gets imprinted in the nervous system with early attachment experiences during the nonverbal stage of development. Repeated ruptures in interpersonal bridges during childhood result in a lowered capacity for right-left brain integration and nervous system regulation into a ventral vagal state.

When situations of shame and trauma continually disrupt activation of the ventral vagal complex, long-term access to the social engagement system decreases, which impacts future relationships. Traumatized individuals carry the disorganized and disrupted states in the body memory, which then keeps the trauma *alive* (Ogden, 2003). Since there is no time in body memory, activating a trauma or shame state can feel as if it is happening in that moment. In turn, clients may engage in a variety of defensive behaviors that reflect their primitive survival instinct. They may strike out in anger, go into a state of immobilization, or engage in other maladaptive coping patterns. Overriding these survival instincts requires retraining the body memory to feel safe.

To help clients regain this sense of safety and return the body to a ventral vagal state, Porges suggests using the four therapeutic R's (Figure 4) when working with trauma and shame: **R**ecognizing the autonomic state the client is in, **R**especting the adaptive survival response, **R**egulating or co-regulating with the client into a ventral vagal state, and then **R**e-storying (Porges, 2009). When the clinician is aware of these four R's in treating shame, the therapeutic dance becomes one of co-regulation and safety. Since shame often hides underground, the clinician needs a very fine level of discrimination while investigating the underlying dysregulated shame states. I will describe each of the therapeutic R's in more detail in chapters 4 through 8.

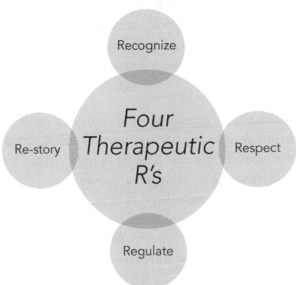

Figure 4. The Four Therapeutic R's

SELF as a Safe Experience of Living Freely

Once we help our clients identify some of these old patterns and start to re-story, it is important to remember that the old somatic memory will often continue to override the new story because the body memory always wins (van der Kolk, 2014). Acronyms are helpful as quick reference points that can bring the new story back to the forefront when the frontal lobe goes offline. As discussed earlier, I often use SELF with my clients to describe a **S**afe **E**xperience of **L**iving **F**reely. We discuss how this is the goal of re-storying and how changing the story might feel awkward and uncomfortable because it is unfamiliar. Keeping the idea of the new story in mind as a safe experience of living freely also helps to frame treatment goals, such as emotion regulation, body memory awareness, freedom of expression, and healthy boundaries.

Additionally, the acronym SAFE can assist clients in working to re-story socioemotional safety by reminding them to **S**elf-source emotional needs, repeat **A**ffirmations, pay attention to **F**eelings as clues, and **E**xpress emotions. Identifying ways to work with these four aspects of safety helps override unconscious repetitions of fear and trains the body to remember more sustainable experiences of safety.

Exercises

The worksheets that follow can help clients begin to address some of the core feelings surrounding not feeling good enough. Keep in mind that using the word *shame* this early on in the therapeutic relationship can itself be shaming for some clients. Therefore, shame is not explicitly mentioned in these worksheets. Instead, phrases such as "not good enough" are used to refer to the core shame affect.

The **Excavation Exercise: Take a Deep SEA Dive** worksheet is a practical tool you can use to identify unconscious shame beliefs, whether or not you used the word *shame* in session yet. So often, clients have been talked out of their feelings and are unable to access what they are experiencing. First and foremost, we want the client to excavate the parts of the self that they may have hidden under their core shame identity. Here we begin the process of re-storying by remembering and reconstructing what the client may have buried in the past.

You can use the **Train Your Puppy to Sit** worksheet to help clients start retraining their core shame beliefs. This represents the first step in the process of re-storying their shame narrative. In my practice, I help clients counteract their "not-enough" beliefs with the metaphor of training a puppy, which is a technique I developed after meeting with a twelve-year-old client who brought her puppy into session one day. She told me she was afraid the puppy would grow too large for her to manage before she was able to train him. As I reflected on how people train puppies, I realized that a similar metaphor was applicable when working with shame. Puppies typically jump up on people without the ability to regulate their excitement. Shame is similar in that it is largely untethered, and anything can trigger it with little warning. Clients can counteract these core shame beliefs and regulate their "shame brain" through the metaphor of training a puppy to sit.

The **Restocking Compassion Chips** worksheet is a simple tool clients can use to help them remember to add more positive affirmations and self-talk to their day. Since the neurobiology of shame is set up early on in the implicit body memory, it often overrides conscious thought, and core feelings of self-doubt and being "not good enough" are usually at the forefront. You can educate clients on how they were born lovable and liken that to a poker chip carousel full of poker chips that reminds them of their authentic truth. Each chip in the carousel represents an aspect of the true self, such as "I am lovable," "I am enough," and "I am worthy of love and belonging." Every time a shaming experience happens, a chip gets taken out of the set. Over time, the carousel becomes empty. This worksheet is a reminder that they can fill the carousel back up again with positive affirmations.

The **SAFE SELF** worksheet further explores the notion of how to self-regulate into a safe experience of living freely and uses the acronym SAFE as a way to provide clients with reminders and tools they can use in the process. Repetition, self-compassion, and nonjudgmental witnessing in this exercise can help shift the old body memories while writing a new story of safety in the body.

Excavation Exercise: Take a Deep SEA Dive

Instruction: Many of us were not raised in families where the free expression of feelings was the norm. We were told things like "Stop crying" or "Don't be angry." As a result, when something triggers us, it can be difficult to uncover our true feelings associated with that event. This exercise helps you get to the heart of the matter and excavate the deeper feelings associated with an event. It allows you to clearly *see* what it is you truly desire.

To excavate your deeper feelings, you can take a deep dive into the SEA by describing the **S**ituation that triggered you, examining your **E**motions related to the situation, and identifying your true **A**spirations in this situation. Each time you recognize a deeper feeling and an aspiration, you discover what you have hidden away. You may have hidden the aspiration because it didn't feel obtainable. Even though it may be out of reach, it is important to allow yourself to *see* it. By using the SEA format, you can bring these unconscious, lost parts of yourself to the surface. Here are the three parts of the SEA:

1. **Situation:** Define what happened in observable, repeatable, and countable terms (e.g., "When you yell at me for not taking out the garbage...") instead of using vague and undefinable language (e.g., "When you are grumpy...").

2. **Emotion:** Search for the underlying emotions associated with the behavior. You can use the **Feeling Words** handout that follows this exercise if you need help identifying your emotions. Try to find words besides *angry*, *frustrated*, or *sad*. Although these words are certainly appropriate, there are usually deeper feelings underneath, such as *attacked*, *unloved*, and *unappreciated*.

3. **Aspiration:** Think of what might have felt better instead and what you truly desire (e.g., "It would mean a lot to me if we could negotiate household chores without yelling and arguing").

For example, combining these three components together, your deep SEA dive might look like this: "When you yell at me for not taking out the garbage (*situation*), I feel attacked and unloved (*emotion*). It would mean a lot to me if we could negotiate household chores without yelling or arguing so much (*aspiration*)."

Excavation Exercise: Take a Deep SEA Dive

Situation: Define the situation in observable, repeatable, and countable terms.

When...

_____

_____

_____

_____

Emotion: Search for the underlying emotion associated with the behavior.

I feel...

_____

Aspiration: Think of what might have felt better instead.

It would mean a lot to me if...

_____

_____

_____

You can make copies of this worksheet to use whenever you want to excavate your true feelings and desires, or you can do this exercise in your journal when something emotional comes up. Although you can also use this exercise secondarily to repair conflict with another person, that is *not* its primary intention. The purpose is for you to take a deep SEA dive to find YOU! Remnants of your authentic self are hidden underneath the surface. Here lies the treasure!

"True wisdom is like an ocean; the deeper you go, the greater the treasures you'll find."
—Matshona Dhliwayo

Feeling Words Chart

Abandoned	Confused	Fulfilled	Needed
Abused	Connected	Full	Needy
Accomplished	Content	Funny	Negative
Adventuresome	Courageous	Gaslighted	Nervous
Alert	Curious	Happy	Offended
Alone	Depleted	Helpful	Organized
Angry	Depressed	Helpless	Out of Control
Annoyed	Directed	Horrified	Overwhelmed
Anxious	Disconnected	Humiliated	Owned
Appreciated	Disliked	Hurt	Patient
Artistic	Dismissed	Included	Peaceful
Ashamed	Disorganized	Inconvenienced	Pensive
Athletic	Dissatisfied	Interested	Pitiful
Awkward	Drained	Involved	Playful
Babied	Edgy	Irritated	Pleased
Beautiful	Elated	Insignificant	Poor
Betrayed	Embarrassed	Invisible	Positive
Bored	Empty	Isolated	Praised
Brave	Energetic	Knowledgeable	Prepared
Broken	Engaged	Lazy	Present
Calm	Enthusiastic	Lethargic	Pressured
Captive	Excited	Lightheaded	Pretty
Centered	Excluded	Lonely	Proud
Challenged	Fabulous	Loved	Pushed
Clumsy	Flattered	Miserable	Put-Upon
Cluttered	Forgetful	Misunderstood	Railroaded
Commanded	Frustrated	Mortified	Relaxed

Restless	Shaky	Surprised	Unaccepted
Rich	Shocked	Sweet	Unappreciated
Romantic	Sick	Talented	Underutilized
Rushed	Silly	Tall	Ungrateful
Sabotaged	Skinny	Thirsty	Unhappy
Sad	Smothered	Thoughtful	Unloved
Satisfied	Spectacular	Tired	Unprepared
Scared	Stressed	Trusting	Used
Scolded	Strong	Ugly	Useless

Others:

_____

_____

_____

Train Your Puppy to Sit

Sometimes, judgment, guilt, fear, and other negative thoughts feel unstoppable, much like a puppy who is not yet trained. Puppies like to jump on people and frantically run around. To train a puppy, the owner must teach it to sit and stay. The only way that the puppy will learn to control its impulses is with constant reminders and cues. Praise for good behavior is also a necessary step in calming the puppy.

Similarly, you can help calm your self-defeating thoughts by identifying them and then counteracting them with a more positive self-acceptance message. In the box on the left, write down a "not-enough" message you might be telling yourself. Then, tell that message to "sit," exhale, and search for a kinder self-acceptance message. Write that message in the box on the right. Quiet your mind by telling the negative thoughts to "sit."

Finally, be sure to encourage yourself for finding a self-acceptance message.

"Not-Enough" Message (e.g., I can't seem to get it right)	Self-Acceptance Message (e.g., I'm doing the best I can)

Restocking Self-Compassion Chips

We are all born lovable. Then, things happen to us that make us feel unlovable. Imagine a poker chip carousel full of poker chips as a newborn baby. Each chip in the carousel represents a truth of who you are: lovable, enough, and worthy of love and belonging. Every time a shaming experience happens, a chip gets taken out of the set. Over time, the carousel becomes empty.

You can fill this carousel back up again by providing yourself with positive affirmations. Every time you notice a self-defeating or self-deprecating thought (e.g., "I never get anything right"), write a positive affirmation (e.g., "I am doing the best I can") in one of the circles.

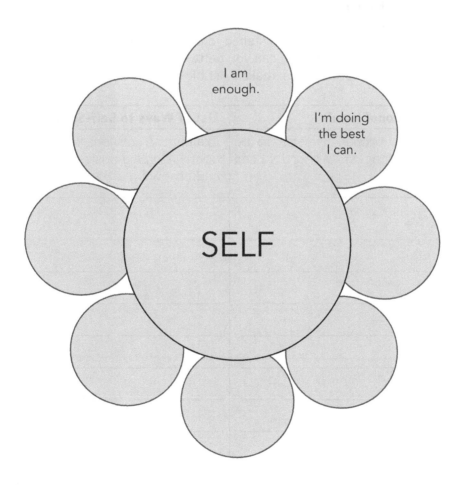

SAFE SELF

Many people have experienced situations in their life where they have not felt seen, heard, validated, or safe. This creates a body memory in the nervous system that can override cognitive thought. This body memory is one of danger that triggers old survival defenses, such as lashing out, running away, blaming, shaming, addiction, perfectionism, codependency, narcissism, rage, and other coping patterns. To change these old defenses, one has to retrain the body memory so it feels safe. Repetition, self-compassion, and nonjudgmental witnessing help shift the old memory so you can begin to write a new story of safety in the body.

To begin creating your own safe experience of living freely (SAFE SELF), think about these four aspects of feeling SAFE to help bring awareness and healing to the body:

1. Self-sourcing emotional needs: We can never go back to change our past. What we can do is discover our unmet emotional needs and find ways to self-source these needs. For example, if you were not heard or listened to as a child, then you might not really be listening and honoring yourself. How can you better listen to yourself? Make a list of your emotional needs in a situation. Then, make a list of ways you can self-source those needs.

Emotional Needs	List of Ways to Self-Source Those Needs
Example: *No one is around to listen to my story. I am feeling alone and unheard. I need to be heard.*	Example: *I can journal, draw, paint, write poetry, or play music. I will listen to myself, and I know I am never truly alone.*

2. Affirmations of safety: Remember that you were born lovable and worthy of love and belonging. What are some affirmations that remind you of that? For example, "I am lovable" or "I am worthy of love and belonging." Write them down and repeat them over and over again to remind the body to change the old story and make room for the new story.

_____

_____

_____

_____

_____

3. Feelings as clues to needs and desires: Many of us have been raised to stop feeling. This creates conflict and incongruency in the body memory. It is important to pay attention to your feelings, acknowledge them, and find a safe place to express them. For example, if you are resentful that your friend has more free time to enjoy her life, pay attention to these feelings and then let them go. Not acknowledging them can result in passive-aggressive or hostile behavior, such as unkind or abusive comments. On the following lines, write down what you are feeling in this situation. Using the **Feeling Words** chart may help you identify them better.

_____

_____

_____

_____

_____

4. Expressing emotions to move old patterns out of the body: All feelings are okay. All behavior isn't. Finding a safe place to express your emotions without hurting yourself or anyone else requires finding a healthy outlet for emotional expression. Some examples of healthy outlets include writing or journaling, engaging in creative arts, or telling a therapist or a safe friend. Moving the energy of the emotion is important to release it from the body memory. List some safe ways you can express your emotions without hurting yourself or anyone else.

_____

_____

_____

_____

_____

3

Empathy in the Therapy Room

"If you put shame in a Petri dish, it needs three things to grow exponentially: secrecy, silence, and judgment. If you put the same amount of shame in a Petri dish and douse it with empathy, it can't survive."

—Dr. Brené Brown

Large Empathy

In the 1990s, scientists discovered neurons that fire in the prefrontal cortex in response to another person's experience, which we now know as *mirror neurons*. For instance, when someone yawns, you also yawn. Or when someone tells you a sad story, you feel sad. Mirror neurons fire automatically during intentional acts and resonate with feelings and all sensory channels. They confirm that we are hardwired to connect (Siegel, 2010). The principal agent of change in treatment is the therapist's capacity for empathy, and mirror neurons are the root of that empathy.

When a client is in a state of shame, there is a loss of a sense of empathy for the self, and the client cannot see others as empathetic either (Jordan, 1997). Shame is healed when the client sees emotional joining and empathy as possibilities. The shame-informed therapist creates the necessary holding environment for the client to experience attuned empathy and coherence in the context of a relationship, which is the missing link in their earlier development.

To do so, the clinician sustains attention while at the same time co-regulating right-brain experiences with clients. Clinicians must call forth the courage to sit with discomfort when feeling with a client—even when the client denies access to their emotional vulnerabilities—and then create a narrative about the bigger picture that explains why the client might be experiencing intolerable feelings of disintegration and shame. This requires what is known as "large empathy" (DeYoung, 2015).

To exhibit this degree of therapeutic empathy, clinicians must "sense a client's anger, fear, or confusion as if it were [their] own, yet without [their] own anger, fear, or confusion getting bound up in it" (Rogers, 1957, p. 284). The clinician's ability to exhibit attunement in the context of the therapeutic relationship is what allows the client to safely describe, contact, and regulate their inner experience (Schore, 2012). It is the key to therapeutic change.

Looking through a lens of core shame and holding an awareness that it may be lurking underground can tremendously inform therapeutic work. Empathy is one of the strongest predictors of client progress, and the ability to be with a client's discomfort is a major part of healing shame. **To co-regulate with clients, clinicians must communicate nonverbal affect, express empathy, use language in personal and engaging ways, and offer emotional sensitivity.** They must tolerate difficult content and encourage clients to navigate uncomfortable feelings. Doing so helps clients to integrate the narrative that they have constructed in their right and left hemispheres, which is needed to regulate core shame.

Being Vulnerable

Working with core shame requires being vulnerable and willing to engage deeply with clients. Throughout the treatment process, clinicians must witness and match the client's affect with curiosity, acceptance, and empathy, all while being respectful and responsive to any indication that treatment is causing anxiety or disconnection. As the therapist empathizes with the client into a state of co-regulation, the therapist's own feelings of shame, such as the imposter syndrome associated with being a fraud or a not "good enough" therapist, might get activated. **Self-awareness is key in navigating these situations and overcoming any barriers to relational presence.**

It is also important to provide opportunities for repair within the therapeutic relationship. Clinicians aren't perfect and may sometimes say or do something that is not clinically appropriate. For instance, if a therapist has a conflict with their spouse or child and then works with a client who speaks about a similar situation, the therapist's anger may get triggered, causing them to be short with the client. Or perhaps a clinician becomes agitated with a client who continues to repeat the same dysfunctional patterns, and they lose safety in the co-regulation process.

Once the clinician recognizes this therapeutic rupture, they might call attention to it. They can apologize and take ownership by saying, "I want to let you know that I reflected on our last session, and I may have not been as present with you as you needed me to be. I want to apologize and repair that with you." This models how to repair ruptures because they most likely were minimally repaired when the client was growing up. In these situations, shame may also emerge for the therapist, as it can activate the imposter syndrome. Clinicians can re-story by reminding themselves that they are doing the best they can and that they are a good enough therapist. No one is perfect.

Ruptures in the therapeutic relationship might also occur owing to a variety of other factors. A client might view a therapist as abusive due to that client's early relational trauma, which can trigger emotional distress that disrupts thinking and puts the client into a dysregulated state (DeYoung, 2015). Additionally, clients can view therapeutic interventions as traumatizing when they trigger memories of an abuser. Even thinking about the past abuser in session can cause the client to view the experience as abusive. Furthermore, when the therapist responds with determination to not fluctuate from a particular therapeutic technique, the client may also see it as an enactment of abuse (Knox, 2013).

Sometimes, even the best intentions can trigger a shame response in a client. Therapeutic empathy requires that clinicians tolerate this right-brain disconnection, pay close attention to how it happened, and take note of which defense mechanisms get activated. Entering a client's dysregulated right-brain affect can threaten self-cohesion. When shame is in the room, therapists may feel discomfort or shut out of the connection (DeYoung, 2015), or they might notice themselves getting defensive or feeling inadequate. These are indicators that the therapist may be getting dysregulated in the session. Bringing awareness to this dysregulation is helpful so the therapist can self-regulate accordingly and return to a ventral vagal state of safety. In working with shame, there is a delicate dance between the therapist and client that involves balancing power, knowing when to name shame, and also being aware that the best intentions can be shaming.

Figure 5. Shame in Clinical Practice
(Lewis, 1988)

In addition, when working with shame, there are five key points to keep in mind as illustrated in Figure 5 (Lewis, 1988). First, identifying the client's feelings of shame in session can lead to greater self-acceptance. This does not imply that therapists must speak the word *shame* but that they simply maintain an awareness of its presence. Second, premature interpretations of content can be shaming. Giving clients too much clinical information and working with the shame narrative too early in treatment can be iatrogenic. Third, because current shame states often give clues to earlier shame, staying with the present experience is helpful. Fourth, resistance following appropriate interventions may indicate shame. Even if the clinician believes an intervention is a good fit, it may trigger core shame in the client. And fifth, it is important for therapists to realize that therapy itself can be shaming due to an imbalance of power. Core shame creates a chronic fear of being exposed as flawed. If a client feels the therapist is above them, it can easily trigger shame.

Balancing Power in the Therapeutic Relationship

Because power differentials can trigger shame, an important part of shame-informed therapy is the clinician's ability to balance power in the relationship. Current treatment models proliferate shame with all-too-common diagnostic tools that refer to mental health issues as "disorders." These models portray the clinician as the "expert," which sets the stage for clients to feel inadequate and, in turn, more easily triggers shame. Balancing power in the relationship requires genuine, nonjudgmental, and curious interactions. Whatever the clinician can do to create a safe environment where the client feels respected and treated as an equal is a helpful contribution to effective shame work.

Ultimately, the role of the clinician is to provide supportive experiences that are nonjudgmental and safe so the client can heal the wounds of the past. Just as caregivers must create a holding environment from which children can grow, therapists must create a safe space that facilitates the development of a trusting therapeutic relationship. This process enhances cortical processing and allows for new neural integration by providing consistent and repetitive opportunities for the client to sculpt new neural pathways necessary for safety and emotion regulation.

You should use caution and discretion when deciding the appropriate time to use the word *shame* when describing the client's experience. The word itself is loaded with various meanings and associations, and naming it might trigger a shame spiral if said aloud too early in the therapeutic relationship. Words such as *not enough*, *fraud*, and *failure* are descriptive of shame and can be good substitutes to use instead. It is important to attune to clients and pay attention to body language, self-deprecating talk, and anxiety so clinicians can gauge when it is appropriate to name shame in treatment. Doing so is like a dance. Clinicians must learn the steps for each individual client and know when to use language that the client may be more comfortable with.

Since empathy is a right-brain experience, it is helpful for clinicians to *feel into* empathy rather than think about what it means. Closing one's eyes and imagining what empathy feels like is one method. Clinicians can also imagine what empathy might say to them if it were to speak (Figure 6).

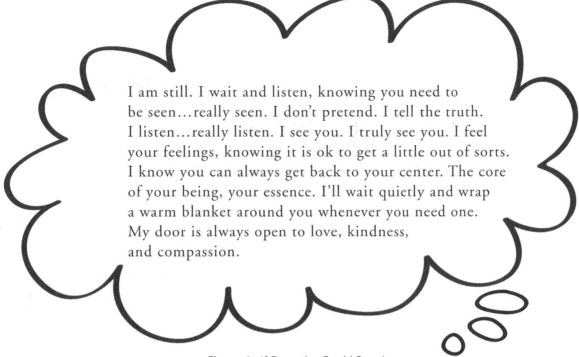

I am still. I wait and listen, knowing you need to be seen…really seen. I don't pretend. I tell the truth. I listen…really listen. I see you. I truly see you. I feel your feelings, knowing it is ok to get a little out of sorts. I know you can always get back to your center. The core of your being, your essence. I'll wait quietly and wrap a warm blanket around you whenever you need one. My door is always open to love, kindness, and compassion.

Figure 6. If Empathy Could Speak

Exercises and Sample Re-Stories

The **Empathy in the Therapy Room** worksheet is a tool geared toward clinicians to help them foster a keener awareness of the multilayered process of therapeutic empathy. What we know now about mirror neurons better explains how and why therapists might get dysregulated during a therapy session. Shame-informed therapists must pay close attention to what they are experiencing while co-regulating with a client. This worksheet helps bring more conscious awareness to what is happening for the therapist, which can then help guide them in fine-tuning the therapeutic process. Therapists can periodically refer back to the worksheet as a reminder of the ongoing parallel process of treatment.

In addition, part of building a strong therapeutic relationship—as well as writing a new story—involves gathering a client's interests and values. Oftentimes, clients who have experienced trauma, abuse, neglect, or failure forget what they truly desire and value. The **Personal Interest Inventory** and **Values** worksheets can assist clients in identifying their interests and values, which will help therapists in finding activities that are well-suited to the client and facilitate building a therapeutic relationship. Both worksheets can inform the therapeutic practices going forward. You can also use these two worksheets with couples. Each partner can fill them out individually for homework, but advise the couple not to share their answers with each other until the next session. Gathering this information helps everyone better understand individual preferences and needs.

Clinicians can also use the **It Wasn't Your Fault** worksheet from chapter 1 to gather parts of the client's story. However, keep in mind the importance of balancing power in the relationship. Too many clinical forms can be intimidating and set the stage for the clinician to appear as the expert, causing the client to feel less empowered in the process. This can trigger core shame as the client experiences the therapist as someone who is more intelligent and more powerful.

Empathy in the Therapy Room: A Self-Assessment Tool for Clinicians

Stepping into the right-brain experience of our clients may present some challenges. Feeling vulnerable, agitated, or frustrated may impact our ability to empathize, and the imposter syndrome can cause us to feel like a fraud and worry about making mistakes. It can also be difficult to sustain connection and hold space if we become triggered by difficult content brought up in session. Here are some thought questions for you to explore in assessing your ability to create a safe and empathic environment. You can always add more as you notice your process of holding space for empathy.

1. What does empathy feel like to you?

_____

_____

_____

2. When a client starts to become dysregulated, how do you feel in your body?

_____

_____

_____

3. What are some clues that a client has triggered your own shame?

_____

_____

_____

4. Is it difficult for you to notice your own shame? How so?

_____

_____

_____

5. What strategies help you self-regulate if you feel triggered in session?

_____

_____

_____

6. Have you noticed any of the following barriers to relational presence recently? In thinking about these barriers, be curious, courageous, and compassionate, and connect to yourself without judgment.

• Lacking self-awareness: _____

_____

_____

• Unconsciously enacting the shaming parent: _____

_____

_____

• Being inflexible: _____

_____

_____

- Having an imbalance of power: _____

  _____

  _____

- Projecting: _____

  _____

  _____

- Having boundary issues: _____

  _____

  _____

- Allowing insurance/diagnosis to dictate treatment: _____

  _____

  _____

"Our shamed clients need changes in how their right brains work for them, but they cannot make these changes on their own. They need to be in sustained connection with at least one other person who is close enough to become someone who can regulate—rather than dysregulate— their right-brain affective experience."

—Patricia DeYoung

Personal Interest Inventory

Circle the activities you enjoy doing, even if these are activities that you have been unable to pursue for some time. Then, list your top three interests at the end of the worksheet. This will help me get to know you better and inform our work together, while helping you find healthy outlets for expressing your feelings.

Team Sports

Basketball   Softball   Baseball   Soccer   Football   Hockey   Bowling   Volleyball

Other (please specify): _____

Engaging in or Observing Individual Sports

Jogging/Running   Tennis/Ping-Pong   Swimming   Bicycling   Walking

Darts   Golf   Horseback Riding   Badminton   Croquet

Fishing   Gymnastics   Boxing   Wrestling   Auto Racing

Other (please specify): _____

Music

Singing   Playing an Instrument   Attending Concerts   Listening to Music

Other (please specify): _____

Dance/Movement

Country   Folk   Square   Aerobic   Yoga   Modern Dance

Tap   Ballet   Jazz   Rock & Roll   Line Dancing

Other (please specify): _____

Arts and Crafts

Painting   Drawing   Knitting   Sewing   Crocheting   Latch Hooking

Embroidery   Weaving   Ceramics   Pottery   Baking   Woodworking

Cooking   Photography   Jewelry Making   Collecting (e.g., stamps, rocks, coins)

Other (please specify): _____

Table Games

Cards   Checkers   Chess   Dominoes   Scrabble   Puzzles

Billiards   Bingo   Board Games

Other (please specify): _____

Outdoor Leisure/Social

Hiking   Climbing   Walking   Gardening   Camping   Skiing

Sledding   Canoeing   Fishing   Roller-skating   Roller-blading   Ice-skating

Boating   Lawn Games   Nature Study   Birdwatching   Barbecues/Picnics

Weather Observation   Amusement Parks/Fairs

Other (please specify): _____

Community Activities

Shopping   Dining Out   Libraries   Aquariums   Museums   Concerts

Parades Flea Markets   Sightseeing   Sporting Events   Hometown Events

Video Games   Going to the Movies   Visiting/Entertaining Friends and Family

Other (please specify): _____

Social Clubs/Organizations

Cultural/Ethnic Clubs   Cooking Clubs   Card Playing   Religious Services

Other (please specify): _____

Literacy/Continuing Education

Reading   Computers   Writing Letters   Taking Adult Education Classes

Other (please specify): _____

Volunteer Work

Political Campaigns   Homeless Shelter   Food Co-op   Special Olympics

Nursing Home   Recycling   Animal shelter

Other (please specify): _____

Top Three Choices:

1. _____

2. _____

3. _____

Values Worksheet

Sometimes, we forget what is important to us when we want to make sure we are doing the right thing and pleasing others. A good way to excavate your true self is to write down what you value. Circle your values on this list. If you think of others, add them to the end. Then, pick your top five and rank them 1–5.

Achievement	Competency	Generosity
Adventure	Contribution	Growth
Authority	Creativity	Harmony
Accountability	Curiosity	Happiness
Ambition	Courage	Honesty
Authenticity	Contentment	Humor
Autonomy	Confidence	Home
Balance	Connection	Health
Beauty	Diversity	Independence
Belonging	Determination	Intuition
Boldness	Equality	Integrity
Compassion	Fairness	Justice
Challenge	Faith	Kindness
Caring	Family	Knowledge
Commitment	Financial Stability	Leadership
Cooperation	Freedom	Learning
Collaboration	Fame	Love
Citizenship	Friendships	Loyalty
Community	Fun	Meaningful Work
		Nature

Openness	Religion	Stability
Optimism	Reputation	Success
Peace	Respect	Status
Pleasure	Responsibility	Time
Patience	Security	Trustworthiness
Power	Self-Respect	Travel
Poise	Self-Expression	Truth
Popularity	Self-Discipline	Vulnerability
Recognition	Service	Wealth
Reliability	Spirituality	Wisdom

Others:

_____

_____

_____

Top 5:

1. _____

2. _____

3. _____

4. _____

5. _____

Sample Re-Story: Empathy (Maria)

Meeting a therapist can be frightening for some, and it can easily trigger shame. For example, Maria was a twenty-one-year-old graduate student studying contemplative psychology. In our second session, she revealed how she was noticing her reaction to my being an older white female. She had the self-awareness and courage to speak to what she was feeling and how it triggered some old memories of moving into an all-white neighborhood in New Jersey as a teen, as well as losing her Middle-Eastern mother to divorce and death at an early age while having to adjust to her Irish stepmother. This was a great opportunity to make the unconscious conscious as we began to rewrite her old story.

(*Note*: Although Maria had enough insight to express what she was experiencing, many clients will have reactions in therapy that may or may not be conscious. Since shame is stored in the implicit memory system and is nonverbal, the clinician must look with a keen eye to assess core shame.)

Old Story: I am not lovable because of my race.

Re-Story: I am lovable just the way I am.

part II

the art and architecture of reconstructing the authentic self

"One of the key practical lessons of modern neuroscience is that the power to direct our attention has within it the power to shape our brain's firing patterns, as well as the power to shape the architecture of the brain itself."

—Dr. Daniel Siegel

4

The Four Therapeutic R's

"The shadow self seems to be the opposite of love. Actually it is the way to love."
—Deepak Chopra

Connecting the Head and the Heart

Integrating the implicit right-brain information with the explicit left-brain narrative requires understanding how the autonomic nervous system responds in relation to core shame. With shame, every action is a reaction in the sake of safety and survival. Specifically, when there are repeated ruptures in interpersonal bridges and minimal capacity for emotional safety, the left-brain narrative often steals the show, causing a disconnect between the head and the heart. These left-brain defenses against shame often result in what is loosely referred to as "monkey mind" because the mind swings from thought-branch to thought-branch with no productive outcome. These thoughts are disconnected from the body memory, or the *heart* of the matter.

These left-brain defenses against shame tend to leave the nervous system in a state of stress because the head and heart are not in coherence. That is because our thoughts influence our emotions, and our emotions directly affect our heart rhythm. Stressful emotions, such as anger, frustration, and anxiety, create irregular and erratic heartbeats, or what is known as an incoherent heart rhythm pattern. This indicates that branches of the autonomic nervous system are out of sync. In contrast, positive emotions, such as appreciation, care, joy, and love, create a coherent heart rhythm that is highly ordered, smooth, and harmonious. It is here that the autonomic nervous system is in sync (Childre & Martin, 2000).

The Four R's

Stephen Porges's (2011) polyvagal theory is a useful model to help clients develop a sense of safety by connecting the head and the heart. In particular, Porges recommends the following four therapeutic R's when working with autonomic nervous system responses in shame and trauma: **R**ecognizing the autonomic state the client is in, **R**especting the adaptive survival response, Co-**R**egulating with the client into a ventral vagal state, and then **R**e-storying (Porges, 2009).

This chapter provides a brief summary of the four R's, whereas chapters 5 through 8 will go into more detail about each individual R and provide suggestions for therapeutic interventions. It is important to keep in mind that the process of co-regulating core shame with a client is nonlinear and sometimes nonlogical because it involves working with the right brain, which comprises affective and often unconscious autonomic nervous system material. Oftentimes, working with shame requires an ability to use the four R's all at once, as the art of integrating the right-brain implicit memory with the left-brain logical thought can be multilayered and complex.

The first therapeutic **R** is *recognizing* the autonomic state the client is in. The clinician is continually looking for clues regarding the client's shame response. For example, if the client is in a dorsal vagal or freeze state, their shame response may involve silence, stiff or rigid affect, nonaction, apathy, and missed appointments. On the other hand, if the client is in a sympathetic or fight-or-flight state, their shame response might show up as anger, defensiveness, or arguing in session. Neither of these states allow for ease of connection or emotional co-regulation. The overall therapeutic goal is to co-regulate with the client into a ventral vagal state of safety and calm.

The second therapeutic **R** is *respect*. Clinicians must respect whatever state the client is in, holding an awareness that this adaptive state has historically served a purpose in the left-brain narrative of safety and survival. Respecting the state doesn't mean it will be comfortable. For example, I was recently training clinicians about Porges's four R's, and a clinician questioned what it means to respect the dysregulated state. She described working with individuals in the criminal justice system who sometimes have no remorse and stated how it was difficult for her to respect that. I explained that respecting the state doesn't mean we have to like it. It simply means respecting where the client is in the moment, knowing it is an adaptive response.

The third therapeutic **R** involves helping the client *regulate* into a ventral vagal state by promoting connection, social engagement, and safety. Doing so requires fine-tuned skills of empathy, compassion, and self-awareness. It involves being able to take perspective, avoid judgment, recognize emotion, and communicate this emotion to others (Wiseman, 1996).

In this co-regulating therapeutic process, the therapist experiences four things all at once: (1) sharing the shame and humiliation of the client; (2) taking on their own perspective while regulating affect when feeling with the client; (3) bearing and containing the experience of being seen, even in instances of projection where the client views the clinician as the abuser; and (4) co-creating a new relational experience where both therapist and client collaborate and co-construct self-compassion (Knox, 2013.) Almost like a hologram, all aspects exist at once (Figure 7).

The fourth therapeutic **R** is *re-storying*. Here the clinician helps the client create a new narrative and provides somatic tools to embody this new story. In the re-storying process, the therapist and client begin to override the story that the client made up in the left brain early on by "editing and expanding the self-narrative of the left hemisphere to include the silent wisdom of the right" (Cozolino, 2002, p. 100). As the clinician and client write a new story—collectively as well as individually—they are working to strip away layers of old patterns, many

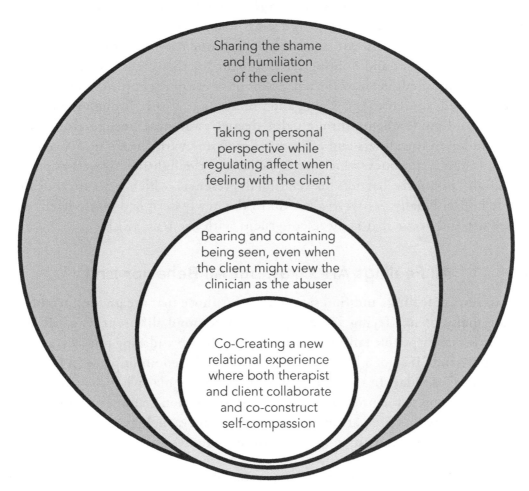

Figure 7. A Hologram of Co-Regulation:
Four Things Happening at Once, Adapted from Knox (2013)

of which live in the unconscious. Because core shame lives mainly in the implicit memory and autonomic nervous system, this process can feel like delving into an unexplored and rather mysterious realm, a type of *twilight zone*. The shame-informed therapist is brave enough to face the shadow material that emerges and co-create a new narrative different from any known before. Imagination is key. I always tell my clients this work is hard because what researchers have discovered about healthy self-esteem and family systems is not what prior generations have experienced; it is mostly unexplored territory.

So many factors affect the therapeutic work with clients that it can help to remember that healing takes time, very much like remodeling a historic house. Rebuilding an old house takes time and patience, and it may require being displaced to a rental home while construction is underway. It can also involve challenges in working with contractors and in deciding what updates to make and what fixtures to choose. Similarly, therapy requires that clients sort out what works and doesn't work for them. It requires a commitment to the self over a period of time and the tenacity to stay with it.

In this respect, it can be helpful to imagine the four therapeutic R's as parts of the reconstruction of a historic house (Figure 8). *Recognizing* the autonomic state the client is in is the foundation of treatment, similar to the foundation and the frame of the house, as it creates a safe container and holding environment for treatment. *Respecting* this autonomic state involves acknowledging how the narratives of safety got set up and how they influence the heart and the head, similar to the wiring and plumbing that run through the house. Therapists then witness and guide clients through this deeper awareness, recognizing that there could be secrets hidden in the closets and cabinets. *Regulating* with clients into a ventral vagal state requires tools and techniques, which we can consider the lighting, as well as paying attention to what might minimize barriers to relational presence, which we can consider the fence around the house. Finally, *re-storying* is akin to the newly designed house itself, compromised of updated art and decor that is more congruent with the true SELF.

All Feelings Are Okay, but All Behavior Isn't

Learning to respect feelings and find safe outlets for those that are uncomfortable is a learning process for many of us. Trying to recognize and respond differently to the elusiveness of emotions leaves many people falling short. Emotionally invalidating phrases, such as "Get over it," "Grow up," and "It's not a big deal," were historically commonplace in families—and still are in some families today. In turn, many adults can't recognize what they are feeling and have little capacity to express themselves to others. Emotions then go underground into the shadow and create behaviors that are part of the core shame story, such as resistance to crying, anger, perfectionism, blaming, and any number of other defenses against shame.

The story I always tell to illustrate the importance of validating feelings is about my now thirty-three-year-old daughter. When she was four years old, she was crying over something that seemed insignificant to the adults in the room, but for her it was important. My mother was visiting at the time and told my daughter to stop crying because she looked prettier when she wasn't crying. My daughter screamed many times louder, and her tearful cry turned into hysterical wailing. I was in graduate school at the time, learning about how we need to validate our feelings. I told my mother that my daughter would stop crying when she was ready. My daughter overheard me and immediately stopped wailing. My daughter simply needed permission to feel her feelings. Talking her out of them was the antithesis of what she needed to regulate her emotional state.

I always tell my clients that *all feelings are okay, but all behavior isn't*. The old parenting paradigm that talked children out of feelings didn't differentiate between the feeling and the behavior. All negative feelings were considered bad, and the behaviors that ensued were thus considered bad as well. Even children who did not grow up with these old parenting practices may have internalized the message that they should bury difficult feelings under the surface, as these messages are still prevalent in today's society. As a result, many individuals have learned negative beliefs about their emotions that simply aren't true. Helping clients access discounted feelings and find appropriate outlets for expression is part of the process of excavating the core shame and writing a new narrative.

Figure 8
Reconstructing the Authentic Self
The Four Therapeutic "R"s
(Building a House)

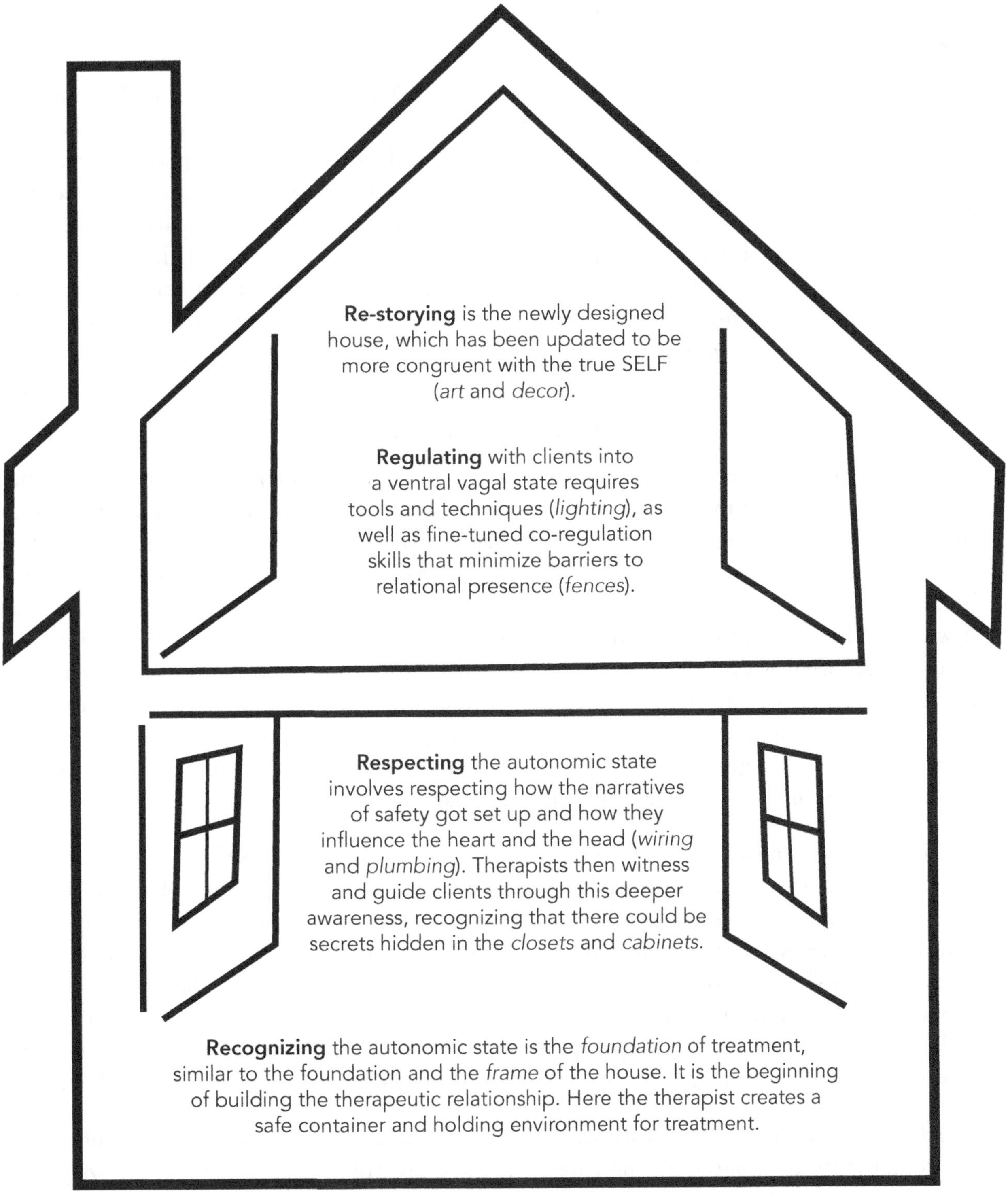

Re-storying is the newly designed house, which has been updated to be more congruent with the true SELF (*art* and *decor*).

Regulating with clients into a ventral vagal state requires tools and techniques (*lighting*), as well as fine-tuned co-regulation skills that minimize barriers to relational presence (*fences*).

Respecting the autonomic state involves respecting how the narratives of safety got set up and how they influence the heart and the head (*wiring* and *plumbing*). Therapists then witness and guide clients through this deeper awareness, recognizing that there could be secrets hidden in the *closets* and *cabinets*.

Recognizing the autonomic state is the *foundation* of treatment, similar to the foundation and the *frame* of the house. It is the beginning of building the therapeutic relationship. Here the therapist creates a safe container and holding environment for treatment.

Working with shame may activate many layers of emotions, and clients may react in unproductive ways when they are put in stressful situations. They may go into a state of immobilization where they judge themselves or avoid others, or they may go into a state of fight-or-flight by lashing out and arguing. **When this occurs, therapists can suggest that clients use four "C" shovels—courage, compassion, curiosity, and connection—that will help them search for tools to change their old patterns.** These tools remind clients to have courage to face the situation, to have compassion for themselves and others, to ask questions instead of making assumptions, and to tap into their innate predisposition for human connection.

Many times, clients hold tight to old anger and don't want to forgive themselves or others. As we excavate shame and look at the subtle and not-so-subtle ways that clients have been wounded or have wounded others, the question of forgiveness comes into play. When allowing clients to feel what they feel when they feel it, forgiveness may take some time. Validating feelings and witnessing the process helps clients eventually come to a place of forgiveness. One of my first supervisors many years ago told me that good therapy is like art. We never know exactly what we will create with the blank canvas. When we trust the creative process and use our imagination, we help our clients paint a whole new story where all feelings are okay, but all behavior isn't.

Embracing Paradox

In Western culture, there is a constant stream of messages from the media portraying images of perfection and happiness as an ideal. This promotes the notion that we should feel good all the time and sets the stage for unrealistic expectations. It also sends the message that we should cut off any feelings associated with sorrow or challenges. However, sadness is a normal part of life, and trying to talk someone out of their feelings can have the opposite effect by making it worse. When individuals attempt to suppress their sadness without allowing themselves to actually feel what they're feeling, this can induce more shame because they'll often find it difficult to quell the emotion. They might wonder why they are unable to "get out of" their depression. Instead, it is more effective to try to help a client pinpoint the source of their grief or depression and to give them permission to feel these feelings. Doing so sometimes lessens the depression, as it is what we resist that persists.

Life is full of joy and sorrow. Learning to embrace that paradox can bring a helpful awareness in treating core shame. A paradox is defined here as two seeming opposites that exist together. If we look closely at our daily life, we can see examples of this paradox when we experience joy and sorrow at the same time. For example, we may feel incredible joy at seeing our child go off to college but simultaneously feel immense sadness at the empty house that comes with their departure. Ultimately, life is a series of pushes and pulls. Something hurts you when you think it shouldn't. You want to do one thing, but you do something else. Most people live somewhere in the middle of this tension of opposites, like a pull on a rubber band (Albom, 1997).

Paradoxes are never resolved. Instead, the lesson lies in embracing paradox. It involves facing the actual truth by digging up the core shame and creating a new story that allows paradox. By embracing paradox and recognizing that opposites are an integral part of life, we strip core shame of its power. Radically accepting, rather than struggling against, negative feelings helps clients to exhale and accept life on life's terms. **Re-storying gives them permission to feel what they feel and to find healthy ways to express emotions.**

Exercises and Sample Re-Stories

The exercises that follow can help clients get back in touch with their feelings, express their emotions in a healthy manner, and embrace paradox. The **Six Ways to Handle Anger** handout provides a reference sheet of ways to manage anger from the least effective to the most effective. Anger in particular is one emotion that has been misunderstood and portrayed as "bad" in our culture, and we are just now learning the difference between anger as an emotion versus healthy outlets for expressing that emotion. **The Six-Step Problem-Solving Process** handout provides a detailed explanation of a problem-solving process that clients can use to most effectively handle anger.

The **Four "C" Shovels** worksheet is designed to give clients tools to excavate more productive ways to manage situations, find a sense of safety, and develop a more effective narrative when challenging or misunderstood emotions emerge. Additionally, the **ABCs of SELF (Safe Experience of Living Freely)** handout is a convenient reference sheet that clients can post nearby as a reminder to use the "C" shovels when they are feeling dysregulated and that all feelings are okay.

The **I Am Sorry That Happened** worksheet helps clients begin the process of forgiving themselves and others. Forgiveness doesn't mean allowing behaviors to continue, but working to let go of the past. Setting healthy boundaries and safe containers for feelings and behavior is always important. Forgiving and letting go can free up energy that might be blocking the flow of joy and creativity.

The final two activities help clients to embrace paradox. Clients can do the **Making a Paradox Box** activity in a group, individually, or as a homework assignment. It addresses all four of the therapeutic R's, as it allows for opportunities to search for paradox and emotional experiences. Additionally, it provides a creative outlet to calm the nervous system through art and helps to re-story outdated narratives with a visual representation of the new story. The **Embracing Paradox in the Heart** activity is a mediation that you can use in session when clients are attempting to make things "all good" or "all bad." Reminding clients that it is always somewhere in between can be a relief as they stop struggling against the "good" versus the "bad" and instead embrace both parts.

Six Ways to Handle Anger

Anger is an energizer. It helps us recognize when we want something to change and helps us better understand what we need. Child development specialist Katharine Kersey, EdD, has created a model of ways to handle anger that range from the least effective to the most effective (Kersey, 1983):

1. **Turning it inward:** The least effective way to handle anger is to turn it inward. This often results in depression and can lead to suicidal thoughts and physical illness.

2. **Lashing out:** A common reaction to anger is to lash out at others physically or verbally. This is an ineffective way to handle anger because it creates more conflict.

3. **Finding a nonproductive outlet:** Anger has a lot of energy that needs to be released. Finding a way to get some of that energy out of the body is a helpful start. This can involve screaming loudly in a safe and appropriate place, hitting a pillow, drawing or scribbling with a black crayon, stomping loudly outside without disturbing others, or any other outlet that can help release the energy but doesn't result in anything productive.

4. **Finding a productive outlet:** This is similar to step 3, but something productive occurs as a result. Examples include working out, running, baking bread, playing the piano, or painting.

5. **Talking about it:** Sometimes, it is helpful to use steps 3 or 4 to release some angry energy prior to talking to the other person about how you are feeling. Once you have calmed down, it is good to have a conversation about how you are feeling without the intensity of the initial anger.

6. **Problem solving:** The most effective way to manage anger is to problem solve, either with the other person or with yourself, so you can identify what the anger is about and what may need to change.

The Six-Step Problem-Solving Process

Engaging others in solving problems helps build connection and better communication skills. You can use this process to manage anger, discuss family challenges, or work out other relationship concerns.

1. **State the problem:** Describe what happened, figure out the problem, and state it. If you can describe the behavior in observable, repeatable, and countable terms, that is the most helpful.

2. **Brainstorm solutions:** Try to think of as many possible solutions to the problem as you can. Don't worry about how "good" they are or whether they will work.

3. **Select one solution:** Think about all the possible solutions you came up with and choose the one you think will work best for solving the problem. Choose a solution everyone can live with that is fair and workable, and that will prevent the same problem from happening in the future.

4. **Implement the solution:** Put the solution into action.

5. **Evaluate the solution:** Evaluate whether the solution is working to solve the problem and whether all parties concerned are satisfied.

6. **Decide:** If it's working, great! Keep it up. If it's not working, go back to step 1 and use the problem-solving process again to figure out another solution that will work, or return to step 3 and select an alternative solution.

Four "C" Shovels

COURAGE COMPASSION CURIOSITY CONNECTION

When we are in a stressful situation, we often react in ways that are not productive. Old stories that don't serve our best interest take over. For example, we might avoid the situation, lash out at others, or turn inward and judge ourselves. The next time you are in a situation and find yourself reacting in a nonproductive way, take a deep breath and use one or more of the "C" shovels to excavate a more effective way to manage the situation. Doing so can help you sort out ways to handle the situation better, find a sense of safety, and write a more productive story.

First, write a summary of a current stressful situation on the following lines:

_____

_____

_____

_____

_____

_____

Then, write some ways that you can use the four "C" shovels to better manage the situation:

Courage: The word *courage* can be traced back to the Latin root *cor*, which is the same root as the word *heart* (coronary). Take a deep breath and ask your heart what it wants in this situation. Make a commitment to listen to your heart and have the courage to love yourself through this situation. What does your heart say? Write it here:

_____

_____

_____

_____

_____

Compassion: The word *compassion* can be traced back to the Latin root *com* (meaning "with" or "together") and *pati* (meaning "to suffer"). Having empathy and compassion for yourself and others can tame fear and help love come to the forefront. What does compassion look like in this situation? How can love lead the way there?

_____

_____

_____

_____

_____

Curiosity: The word *curiosity* can be traced back to the Latin root *cura* (meaning "care and concern"). Imagine yourself as a young child, full of wonder and awe. Ask questions. Never make assumptions about the situation. Be curious. What are some questions you can ask yourself about this situation? What are some questions you can ask of others?

_____

_____

_____

_____

_____

Connection: The word *connection* can be traced back to the Latin root *com* (meaning "together") and *nectere* (meaning "to bind or tie"). We are biologically wired for connection. The most important connection being to ourselves. Take a deep breath and connect to yourself. Give yourself permission to be with you. Then, ask yourself what you can do to connect to others involved.

_____

_____

_____

_____

_____

ABCs of SELF
(Safe Experience of Living Freely)

✓ **Acknowledge feelings:** All feelings are okay. All behavior isn't. Give yourself permission to feel what you are feeling without judgment or talking yourself out of these feelings. Don't react. Instead, take a few deep breaths and then choose one or more "C" shovels to find a more productive solution.

✓ **Breathe:** When we are in a stressful situation, we tend to take shallow breaths. This doesn't allow enough oxygen to get to the brain and the nervous system. The body needs oxygen to help regulate our emotions. Deep belly breaths help start off the process of feeling safe in SELF.

✓ **"C" shovels:** Once you have acknowledged your feelings and taken a few belly breaths, use one or more of the "C" shovels to shift perspective and deepen your sense of safety in the moment.

> **1. Courage:** Be brave.

> **2. Compassion:** Have a heart.

> **3. Curiosity:** Ask questions.

> **4. Connection:** Get in touch with yourself and others.

I Am Sorry That Happened

We all have had bad things happen to us. Sometimes bad things were done to us, and sometimes we did bad things. The things that happened were choices. When we can see them as mistakes and not as complete pictures of who we are or who the other person is, we can move into forgiveness. But forgiveness doesn't mean allowing the behavior to continue. It's also important to set appropriate boundaries and to create a safe container where we can express feelings and behavior in a healthy manner. In this process of forgiving and letting go, we can free up energy that might be hampering our creativity or impeding our joy.

Make a list of people whom you might need to forgive and why. Next, make a list of the things you need to forgive yourself for and possibly with whom you might need to make amends (if doing so does no harm).

People I Want to Forgive and Why	What I Want to Forgive Myself For	People I Might Need to Make Amends With

Making a Paradox Box

Paradoxes are never resolved. Instead, the lesson lies in embracing paradox. Although Western culture often sends the message that we should strive for happiness and repress emotions associated with grief or sadness, this is unattainable because life is full of ups and downs. Embracing paradox involves allowing these emotions to coexist by finding joy in the face of challenge and grief. For example, we can grieve the loss of a grandparent who had been suffering with Alzheimer's for over twenty years, while simultaneously feeling relief that the pain, suffering, and struggle is complete.

This exercise is a creative reminder of how holding paradox can be restorative. To embrace paradox, it helps to contain the energy of the opposites in a way that allows you to express emotions in a safe manner, instead of repressing them. The paradox box allows for creative expression and is also a reminder of ways to contain the opposites.

Materials Needed:

- Small pieces of paper
- A small cardboard box
- Old magazines
- Scissors
- Colored markers
- Optional: embellishments like ribbons or beads

Directions:

1. On small pieces of paper, write down some paradoxes you experience, with one opposite on each side. For example, "I am happy when my son goes snowboarding. I am worried my son could get hurt snowboarding."

2. Think of ways you can contain the paradox, and cut out pictures and words from magazines that describe them, such as meditation, yoga, healthy foods, or rest.

3. Glue the pictures and words to the box. You can also add ribbons, beads, or other embellishments you might have on hand.

4. Place the small pieces of paper in the box and keep the box in a place where you can easily see it as a reminder of how you embrace and contain paradox.

Embracing Paradox
in the Heart

Sometimes, we try to judge a situation as "all good" or "all bad." Yet most of the time, both positive and negative elements exist simultaneously. Being able to embrace both parts and bring more love into the heart can ease the pain. This meditation helps you to embrace paradox and to bring more love into your experience, whether it is primarily positive or negative.

Take a few deep breaths, relaxing your body.

Exhale out any tension you might be holding, and on the inhale, breathe in safety and relaxation.

Just be with your breath for a few moments here.

As you feel yourself relax, with your hands by your side, imagine that you are holding your current situation, one of stress or sadness, in your right hand.

In your left hand, imagine holding hope and self-compassion for the experience.

Hold both parts in your hands by your side.

Now, place what it is you are holding in your right hand over your heart. Then, take the hope and self-compassion in your left hand and place it on top of your right hand.

Hold them both there for a few minutes, and as you breathe in, trust that all is well in this paradox.

Love both parts, the good and the bad, and know that you are safe.

Sample Re-Story: Embracing Paradox (Kelly)

Kelly was a sixteen-year-old who struggled with anxiety and depression. When we discussed art and other activities that might help her regulate her emotions, she reported worrying about the consequences of not allowing herself to fully feeling her uncomfortable feelings. I explained that our negative feelings are like the garbage in our homes. It is going to be there, whether or not we want it. Our job is to find a container to hold these feelings until we can let them go.

Embracing the paradox for her in this case was being able to find some joy in creative expression and playfulness, while at the same time recognizing that she had feelings that she needed to attend to, contain, and acknowledge.

Old Story: I can't feel good and bad at the same time.

Re-Story: I can embrace the paradox of joy and sadness. All my feelings are okay.

Sample Re-Story: Four "C" Shovels (Karen)

Karen was a forty-two-year-old mother of two children, ages five and seven. Growing up, Karen was often yelled at as a child, and she was afraid her children would grow up and experience the same feelings of disappointment and chronic shame she had felt most of her life. Although she had studied and implemented new parenting strategies, she was frustrated that her husband ignored her suggestions and continued to use punitive punishment, yelling at and scolding the children when they misbehaved. Her continual demanding that her husband parent differently hadn't been effective in helping him understand the importance of her newfound parenting style.

I suggested that she use the four "C" shovels in her interactions with him. Using *curiosity* to ask her husband questions rather than demanding he change, finding the *courage* to face the inner sadness triggered by her memories, and *connecting* with her husband with more *compassion*. Using the "C" shovels helped her to recognize how much she wanted to alleviate the pain she suffered as a little girl by sheltering her children. Karen was also able to come to the realization that her children were able to articulate how they felt, which she was never able to do as a child.

Old Story: I have to shelter my children to protect my own pain.

Re-Story: I am parenting differently from how my parents raised me, and I am a good enough mother.

5

RECOGNIZE Shame Hidden Behind the Story

"While terror and distress hurt, they are wounds inflicted from outside which penetrate the smooth surface of the ego; but shame is felt as inner torment, a sickness of the soul."

—Silvan Tomkins

Safety and Trust

The early stages of work with a client are delicate. You get the call and set up an intake appointment with only a small amount of information. The client doesn't know much about you, and you know little about your client. The dance of safety and trust begins here. It is the foundation of the work, much like building the foundation and frame on a new house.

Establishing parameters at the beginning of treatment helps to set the stage for safety. Letting clients know what to expect facilitates building a strong foundation. For example, many clients want to know how long therapy takes. That question is subjective and difficult to answer in the first session. Pointing out the many years it took to set up familiar patterns is a good way to explain why therapy is a commitment to the self that might take some time. If possible, regularly scheduled weekly sessions are preferable to help create a body rhythm for the work together and contribute to building safety and trust.

When we look at a client through the lens of shame-informed therapy, we may recognize things that otherwise would have remained hidden. Clients' defenses against shame vary based on the narrative that developed early on. **A shame-informed clinician will always be looking through the lens of implicit memories to identify clues that might indicate core shame in the therapy session.** Some clues may include those that are *paralinguistic* (e.g., subtle elements of speech, such as hesitation, soft speech, silences, rapid speech, mumbling, stammering), *verbal* (e.g., words that the client may use, such as *foolish, silly, ridiculous, shy, idiotic, stupid, humiliated,* and *embarrassed*), and *nonverbal* (e.g., body language that the client may exhibit, such as covering their face, looking down, fidgeting, hunching, biting lips, averting gaze)(Retzinger, 1995). Always having a watchful eye for signs of shame helps the clinician stay within the four therapeutic Rs, particularly in terms of recognizing shame hidden behind the story.

A sensitive therapist can listen for the implicit story beneath the ordinary autobiographical stories that clients tell. A client's experience of depression, anxiety, exhaustion, or fragmentation can provide glimpses into the right-brain story behind the left-brain one they more easily tell. The wordlessness of shame and the autonomic response it arouses, such as sweating, increased heart rate, and blushing, makes it a primitive reaction that opposes rational solutions (Lewis, 1988), which makes it difficult to recognize.

Attachment Styles

Since shame is a nonverbal, visceral response to acute misrecognition or misattunement with others, being able to recognize a client's attachment style can help clinicians get a sense of how core shame might present in therapy. Keeping an eye out for these attachment styles can help clinicians navigate effective ways to create safety. For example, individuals with *avoidant attachment* tend to have a strong sense of independence. They may have grown up with few emotionally nurturing caretakers and, in turn, developed a story of having to do things on their own. They may be critical of the therapist and may not feel they need any help.

A few examples of how avoidant attachment might present in the therapy room are: hesitation to start therapy and only doing so after a major crisis or loss, wanting to know details of the clinician's credentials, and minimizing comments (such as "I don't really need to be here," "Everyone else has bigger problems than I do," "I'm only here so you can help me fix my daughter," and "I'm fine"). The left-brain narrative they reveal is often full of missing parts and is very factual, with little emotion. Adding playfulness might help these clients to relax, to not take the session too seriously, and to begin to build trust (DeYoung, 2015). Making appropriate and non-shaming jokes, playing therapeutic games, talking about sports, or using other lighthearted approaches can help the clinician build a relationship with avoidant-attachment clients.

In contrast, clients with *disorganized attachment* tend to struggle with maintaining relationships. They may have grown up with unpredictable or frightening parents. In turn, they have difficulty regulating their emotions and exhibit problems with dissociation, panic, and intense fear. Clients who exhibit disorganized attachment might cancel or miss appointments, show up late to session, worry about not getting better quickly and disappointing the therapist, or fear that the therapy process might be punitive or punishing. The left-brain narrative these clients tell is often chaotic, fragmented, and emotional. When clients are characterized by disorganized attachment, it is best to provide a soothing and calming environment (DeYoung, 2015). For example, clinicians can offer soft lighting, comfortable seating, hot tea, or calming artwork.

Finally, clients with *ambivalent attachment* typically have grown up with parents who were inconsistently attuned to them as children—sometimes nurturing and fully present, and sometimes insensitive and emotionally unavailable. As adults, these clients may be characterized by confusion, insecurity, distrust, or suspicion. In the therapy session, clients with ambivalent attachment may abruptly change how they react to the therapist (oscillating from praise to criticism), exhibit anger at the therapist when setting boundaries, and accuse the therapist of being unkind. Their left-brain narrative might be pressured and preoccupied, containing a lot of words, and it's often disorganized and lacks boundaries of the past and present. In this case, the therapist must be prepared to quickly adjust to unpredictable changes in affect and mood (DeYoung, 2015).

Regardless of whatever adult attachment style might be lurking underground, paying attention and having sensitivity can help the clinician better enter into the right-brain dysregulated affect. By providing empathy for the confusion, anxiety, or emptiness clients have felt, clinicians can help clients connect to some of the vulnerable ruptures of their nonverbal early years.

In addition, offering some cognitive stories to demystify shame can build safety early on in the therapeutic relationship. Alice Miller's *For Your Own Good* (1983), Bruce Lipton's *The Biology of Belief* (2005), and Bessel van der Kolk's *The Body Keeps the Score* (2014) are a few suggested books if clients are interested in reading more about how the common experience of feeling "not good enough" gets encoded in the body and the subconscious. It might also be helpful to present the notion of transgenerational trauma, explaining how trauma can be passed down across generations through ancestral DNA, to help clients see that it's not just about the personal self but a larger collective impression that got imprinted long ago. Providing this psychoeducation helps demystify the experience for clients.

Familiar Confabulations

After the age of seven or eight, most of what we believe to be true is already established in our implicit memory. For example, children who were taught that crying is bad or that wealth is the only measure of success come to accept those as personal truths. It is almost as if they are walking around in a hypnotic trance (Lipton, 2005). Clients may feel that their heart and head are being driven by incongruent messages, yet they don't question them because it is all they know.

These messages represent a type of confabulation because the underlying message is distorted and deceptive, but the individual who presented this information did not do so with the intent to deceive the client. Rather, confabulating individuals believe that the information they are communicating is accurate and sincere (Brown et al., 2017). For example, parents who tell their children that the only way to succeed in life is to go to a very well-regarded college are not trying to deceive their child. They are simply expressing their personal belief, which the child then internalizes as truth. However, if the child grows up and decides not to go to college, shame might get activated when the adult child attempts to separate from the family story that equates success with a college education. Internal feelings of disappointment, failure, and being not good enough may lurk underground.

Giving clients permission to identify and challenge these familiar confabulations, or what we might call confabulated "family lies," is an important step in treating core shame. Teasing out the confabulations for each individual client can help decode the old story and identify core shame. During this process, clinicians might find it helpful to point out that the words *family* and *liar* are present in the word *familiar*, as this sets the stage for identifying patterns and mistaken truths.

Mindfulness and Meditation

Oftentimes, clients who harbor core shame will find themselves in a dysregulated state that involves "what if-ing." Clients imagine all the possible things that might go wrong because they believe it will somehow protect them from facing vulnerability, dealing with failure, or being exposed as flawed. They rehearse vulnerability to try to avoid any possible bad things from occurring. The truth is bad things happen to everyone. None of us are exempt. And most often, it is the tragedies that we never predict that actually happen.

Two examples of the many what-if questions clients might ask themselves are "What if my parents don't talk to me anymore if I tell them how I feel?" and "What if my friend is upset if I tell her the truth?" This fear response is based on old experiences of being abandoned and feeling unloved or unsafe. It is not based in present reality. Therefore, coaching clients to be with "what is" instead of "what if-ing" is a good tool to help them stay in the present moment and return the nervous system to a state of calm.

Bringing clients into the present moment is an ongoing process of psychotherapy. To do so, you can introduce mindfulness practices early on in treatment, which involve helping clients develop a "moment-to-moment nonjudgmental awareness" (Kabat-Zinn, 2005). When clients are in the present moment and not in judgment, they are able to activate the part of the brain that helps them regulate their emotions and feel better about themselves.

Not only can mindfulness meditation increase self-compassion and reduce proneness to shame (Keng & Tan, 2017; Woods & Proeve, 2017), but it's also been shown to have positive effects on depression and anxiety. Neuroimaging studies have even found that meditation experts exhibit neural changes that persist beyond the meditative task itself, suggesting that consistent mindfulness practice can result in long-term changes in empathy, health, and metacognition (Gundel et al., 2018).

However, in our ever-busy world, it can be challenging for clients to take large amounts of time for mindfulness meditation. Many clients report that they simply don't have time. Indeed, setting aside time to engage in formal meditation practice can be more time intensive, so clinicians can instead suggest that clients take several small mindful moments per day to help calm the mind and tame the shame spirals. For example, clients can find a minute to be mindful while taking a shower, driving their car, sitting outside in nature, or walking the dog. They can also cultivate an attitude of mindfulness by drawing their attention to the breath— focusing on each inhale and exhale—so they can let go of any thoughts and reground in the present moment.

Some clients may also find it useful to download relaxation and meditation apps on their smartphones, such as Calm©, Head Space©, and Mindful©. Shakti Gawain, Jon Kabat-Zinn, and many other meditation teachers have audio and written versions of guided meditations as well. Encourage clients to play around and find something that resonates with them. For example, Head Space offers a guided imagery sleep meditation where clients can choose from a variety of calming experiences, such as a walk in the mountains or on the beach. Many clients report that it calms their mind and helps them sleep. Guided imagery is particularly useful for clients who have difficulty quieting their mind, as it helps direct their thoughts into calming visualizations, which leaves less space for the mind to wander into worry, shame, and doubt.

Inspirational card decks are another great way to bring clients back into the present moment and give them an image or a thought to help them stay focused on the new narrative. Many are available now with different themes, such as *The Self-Compassion Deck* (Willard, Abblett, & Desmond, 2016) and others. I have several bowls of different ones in my office. Often, a client will randomly pick one, and it helps them calm down and reground in the moment.

Walking meditations can be useful as well because moving the body helps activate the nervous system and allows the client to step more fully into healing through the rhythm of walking. Some therapists may even find it beneficial to conduct therapy while taking a walk with their client. Labyrinths also provide a more defined walking meditation and can be used with the intention of healing core shame. When starting to walk a labyrinth, the client can hold an intention to be open to feeling good enough and to let go of shame. The process of walking the maze-like circle path takes clients in and out from the center to the edge. Sometimes, they're close to the center, but then a few steps later, they're back on the outer edge. It's a walk of faith and patience, as well as a mindfulness practice that brings clarity and guidance.

In her book *Crossing to Avalon*, psychologist Jean Shinoda Bolen wrote about her experience of walking the labyrinth this way: "We find what really matters to us and can reach the core or center of meaning in ourselves, which is the center of the labyrinth, and then we have the task of integrating this into what we do with our lives when we emerge" (1994, p. 163).

Exercises and Sample Re-Stories

Our job as clinicians is to help clients come into present-moment awareness. To facilitate this process, the following section contains several exercises you can use with clients to help them demystify shame and become more present and mindful in the current moment. The **What's Familiar** worksheet helps clients bring to consciousness some of the family confabulations that they were told. Recognizing these lies helps create a more authentic SELF story. This worksheet can also be used as a clinical assessment tool instead of being given to the client if it appears that doing so would be too triggering or overwhelming. The **What Is?** worksheet is a tool to help clients remember to stay present and not think too far into the future. Focusing on "what is" allows the body to feel safe in the present while finding something true about the current situation.

Two meditations are also offered—**I Am Enough** and **The Wisdom Rock**—which you can use as guided imagery exercises in the office. Finally, **The Art and Architecture of Reconstructing the Authentic SELF: RECOGNIZING the Autonomic State** worksheet can help clients assess their SELF, or safe experience of living freely, and recognize what they can do when they are not feeing emotionally safe.

What's Familiar

The word *familiar* contains the words *family* and *liar*. Many of the familiar stories we learn early on about ourselves are not true, nor are they in our conscious awareness. Some examples of these "familiar" messages you might have been given include: "I must do what my family wants me to do," "I'll never amount to anything," or "Being successful means having money."

This worksheet will help you excavate some of the familiar lies you may tell yourself. Recognizing these lies will help you know how to create a more authentic SELF story. Answer the questions here or in your journal if you need more space. Take as much time as you need with each question. You can always add to the list and journal more about each question as time goes by and deeper layers are discovered. This is not an easy exercise. Be patient with yourself and the process.

1. What are some of the lies you learned in your family?

_____

_____

_____

_____

_____

_____

2. When did you realize something was a lie? How old were you? What event precipitated this realization?

_____

_____

_____

_____

_____

_____

3. How has the lie impacted your belief about your SELF?

_____

_____

_____

_____

_____

_____

4. How else have family lies affected your life?

_____

_____

_____

_____

_____

_____

5. What might be different if you were able to be your authentic SELF?

_____

_____

_____

_____

_____

What Is?

When you are feeling stressed, it's not uncommon to go through a long list of hypothetical what-ifs in your mind. However, trying to feel safe by having a plan for every what-if takes a lot of time and energy. Instead, focusing on "what is" allows your body to feel safe in the present moment. It allows you to find something true about the current situation, breathe into what is, and let the rest go. The following are some examples of how to combat what-ifs by reminding yourself of what is.

What if: Teresa frequently worries about what other people think of her. She wonders if she should go to a party in the neighborhood. She starts to think about all the people she might see and what they might say to her that will trigger her feelings of being unlovable. What if they say things behind her back? What if they think she is odd? She starts to go through these various what-if scenarios so she can predict how she will respond.

What is: Teresa is a good friend. She is enough.

What if: John is getting a divorce. He wonders how the children will cope with the divorce and what they might think of him as a father. He goes through all the what-ifs that could happen in his children's lives. What if they are depressed? What if he can't afford to take them on vacation?

What is: John is a good father. He is doing the best he can.

Now it's your turn. Use the following lines to write your what-if statement (e.g., "I am a bad mother and my children will grow up with anxiety"), and then follow it up with a what-is statement that demonstrates the truth (e.g., "I am a good mother, and I am doing the best I can"). Then, breathe and let the rest go.

What if...

_____

_____

_____

What is...

_____

_____

_____

I Am Enough Meditation

Get into a comfortable position, either lying or sitting down with a straight spine. Close your eyes or look at a spot in front of you with a soft gaze, whatever feels best to you. Now take a deep breath in that fills your lower abdomen, and then exhale any stress you might be holding in your body. Just let it go. Take a few more deep breaths, inhaling all the way down into your lower belly and exhaling tension.

Now bring your awareness to your feet. Feel your feet on the ground. Wiggle your toes. Roll your ankles. Feel your feet become part of the earth. Now bring your awareness to your calves and any tension you might be holding there. Let that tension roll down into your feet, your toes, and down into the earth as you continue to breathe in and out. Feel your knees and your hips. Notice any tension you might be holding in those areas and let it all roll down into the earth. Notice your belly, your lower back, and your chest. Breathe in and then slowly exhale. Release whatever stress you are holding there. Notice your upper back and your arms, hands, and fingers. Shake all the tension out.

Now bring attention to your face, your jaw, and your eyes. Inhale and exhale. Notice your scalp, your forehead, and the back of your neck. Breathe into those areas. Now let go of any thoughts or worries on your mind. There is no need to worry or stress. Everything in this moment is exactly as it should be.

Now imagine you are walking down a path. Take rhythmic, slow, and easy steps, counting one, two, three, four as you walk. And as you continue down the path, you approach a bridge. Walk over the bridge with the same slow and easy steps, counting one, two, three, four, until you land on the other side. From this point, you can continue to walk slowly until you find a place that you might want to stop and explore in a different way. Take a minute to see what is there. This place belongs only to you. Here you feel like you belong and like you are enough. Use childlike curiosity and wonder to explore this place for little while. Are there animals? What sounds, people, or things do you recognize? Have the courage to explore what surrounds you. There may be a door, another path, a cave, or water. This is your space. Notice any colors or shapes you might see. Give yourself time to look around.

Walk around one more time to see if there is anything else that is important for you to discover in this place where you are enough. Thank this place and everything you were able to explore for giving you this experience and say goodbye for now. You can always come back to your special place of being enough whenever you so choose.

Now turn around and start walking back to the bridge with your rhythmic, slow, and easy steps, counting one, two, three, four. And when you arrive on the other side, continue your path until you feel yourself come back into the room. When you're ready, open your eyes. You can write or draw any images, colors, thoughts, or things that you explored if you choose.

The Wisdom Rock Meditation

Close your eyes and imagine you are surrounded by rocks. They have been there for many years and are holding the ancient wisdom of the earth. Water may have smoothed them a bit, and now they lay steady, still, and strong in front of you. Take a few deep breaths and thank the rocks for being here for you. Imagine that each of the rocks has a word carved into it, such as *courage, compassion, curiosity, vulnerability, faith, trust, love, playfulness, honesty, miracles, blessings*, or any other word that may have been placed there just for you.

Now look around at the rocks and pick the one you feel most called to. Perhaps you like the shape, the color, or the word. Simply pick the one you want to hold in your hand for a moment.

Hold the stone in your hand and feel the essence of the word on the stone. What does it mean to you? How is this word going to inform you about your true self? What else does this wisdom stone want you to know? Be with the stone for a few minutes and allow the answers to come. Take as much time as you need to be with your stone.

Once you feel complete, thank the stone for the wisdom it has revealed to you. Look at it and feel it in your mind, and then find a safe place to toss it. Perhaps you are by a river, a lake, or an open space. Throw it into the space and reflect on the lessons it has taught you. If you threw it into water, you may notice a ripple effect. Know that the wisdom of this rock extends out into your life and the world around you.

You can always come back to this word again when you need to. You also can come back to this sacred space again and ask for another word and repeat this meditation. For now, open your eyes and continue with your day, holding the wisdom of your rock.

Reconstructing the Authentic SELF:
RECOGNIZING the Autonomic State
(Foundation and Frame)

Comparing the foundation and frame of a house to a safe container for developing a SELF, this worksheet can be used as a guide to help you identify ways to feel emotionally SAFE. Similar to the SAFE SELF worksheet on pages 34 & 35, this exercise helps you explore the following questions:

- How can you **S**elf-source your emotional needs?

- What are some of your **A**ffirmations of safety?

- What are some **F**eelings you recognize when you don't feel emotionally safe?

- How can you **E**xpress those feelings?

Self-sourcing emotional needs: We can never go back to change our past. What we can do is discover our unmet emotional needs and find ways to self-source them. For example, if you were not heard or listened to as a child, then you might not really be listening to and honoring yourself. How can you better listen to yourself? On the following worksheet make a list of ways you can self-source your needs where it says "I can **self-source** my needs by...". For example: I can self-source my needs by journaling, drawing, painting, writing poetry, etc.

Affirmations: Remember that you were born lovable and worthy of love and belonging. On the following worksheet write an affirmation that reminds you of that where it says" Today's affirmation of safety is..." For example: I am lovable, I am worthy of love and belonging, etc.

Feelings as cues: Pay attention to what you are feeling. Many of us have been raised to not feel our feelings. Yet, all feelings are okay. Give yourself permission to acknowledge your feelings. Paying attention to feelings allows you to let them go. On the following worksheet write down any feelings you might be having where it says "Today I feel..." For example: Today I feel sad and lonely.

Expressing emotions: Finding a safe way to express emotions without hurting yourself or anyone else requires first recognizing feelings. The next step might be writing about them, and/or telling a therapist or a safe friend. Writing, drawing, or moving the energy of the emotion is important to release it from the body memory. On the following worksheet, you can circle one or more of the ways you might want to express your feelings where it says "I can express my feelings by..."

Reconstructing the Authentic Self
RECOGNIZING the Autonomic State
(Foundation and Frame)

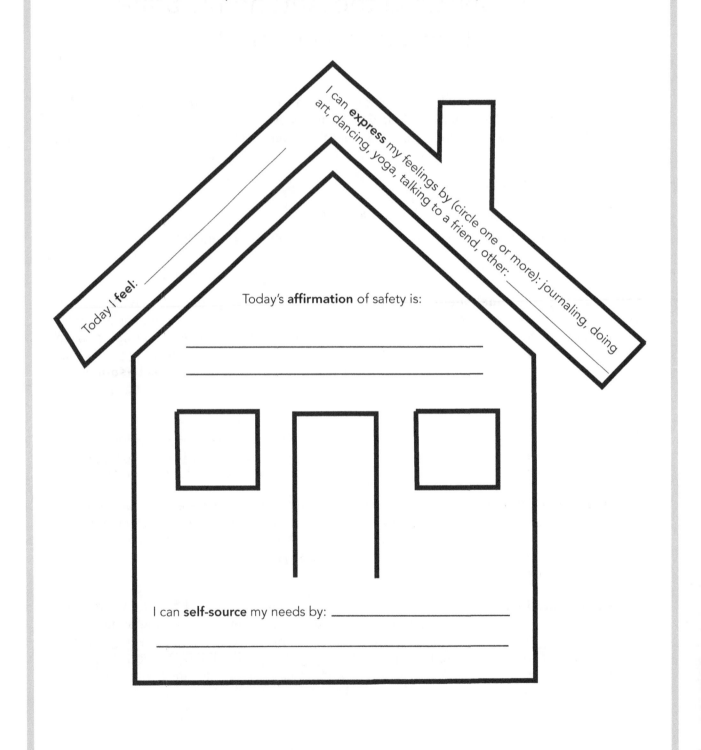

I can **express** my feelings by (circle one or more): journaling, doing art, dancing, yoga, talking to a friend, other: _____

Today I **feel**: _____

Today's **affirmation** of safety is:

_____
_____

I can **self-source** my needs by: _____
_____

RESPECT How the Story Creates The Illusion Of Safety

"A primary tool across all models of psychotherapy is editing and expanding the self-narrative of the left hemisphere to include the silent wisdom of the right."

—Dr. Louis Cozolino

Finding Cohesion

The left-brain narratives that clients develop are mechanisms for survival. Every action is a reaction in the sake of safety and survival. The left brain provides organization and a logical interpretation of things, but the right brain holds the emotions and the contextually coherent meanings regarding social engagement and relationships (Siegel, 2007). Clients with core shame carry those unconscious meanings into everyday life as they then attempt to cope with feeling unworthy of love and belonging by using the left-brain narratives they developed early on.

These clients struggle to form a coherent sense of self because core shame is embedded deep within their neurobiology. Instead, a chronic disintegration of self makes them feel, empty, shattered, or easily humiliated (DeYoung, 2015). Clients who carry shame often have a history of being left on their own to repair ruptures when there has been a situation of conflict or distress. They are deserted and left to recover on their own. This feeling of not being connected or recognized is what leads them to develop a disintegrated sense of self. And when clients maintain this disintegrated sense of self, they view any future relationship ruptures (real or imagined) as dysregulating and possibly a threat to self-cohesion (DeYoung, 2015).

Better understanding how the story created an illusion of safety allows the clinician to *respect* how core shame created this sense of disintegration in relationship to the other. The therapist can then appreciate how the client's defenses were merely created in an attempt to offset the core shame. **Whether clients are avoidant, dependent, disorganized, or defensive, respecting this behavior as a coping mechanism can help the clinician feel empathy, which is the antidote to shame.**

The empathy of the nonverbal attuned response from a shame-informed therapist eases the visceral feeling of shame, even when the shame is unspoken. The therapeutic relationship provides a new shared experience that respects the client's capacity for integration, vitality, freedom, and inner peace (Kohut, 1984). This internal ability for the therapist to see the client as whole even when they are dysregulated or disintegrated provides a solid foundation for healing core shame and allows the client to develop a more coherent self-experience (Kohut, 1984).

As clinicians build relationships with their clients, they are continually gathering information about the confabulations and familiar patterns that were created early on and how they continue to show up throughout a person's life. Respecting these adaptive survival responses informs the client and therapist about the reason why it might take a while to change them. These stories are sometimes difficult to tell. As the therapist respects where the client is, the story emerges in its own time (Figure 9).

> ## "There is no greater agony than bearing an untold story inside you."
>
> -Maya Angelou,
> *I Know Why the Caged Bird Sings*

Figure 9

Moving Away, Moving Toward, or Moving Against

There are three typical responses to shame: (1) moving away, which includes behaviors such as isolation and avoidance; (2) moving toward, which involves people pleasing, codependency, and over-giving; (3) and moving against, which manifests as lashing out, fighting back, or hurting others. We can easily view these shame responses through the lens of the polyvagal theory by considering how they reflect different states of autonomic nervous system activation.

For example, *moving away* reflects activation of the dorsal vagal complex, the oldest and most primitive response of the autonomic nervous system, which is associated with immobilization or a "freeze" response (Dana, 2018). People in this state may become detached, hopeless, and withdrawn. In contrast, *moving toward* and *moving against* reflect activation of the sympathetic nervous system, which mobilizes the body to take action. People in this state can either move toward by going above and beyond expectations to try to make everyone happy, or they can move against by lashing out and being aggressive.

The goal is to help the client return to a state of connection and safety by activating the ventral vagus complex, or the social engagement system as it is commonly known. Activating the ventral vagus nerve provides the way out of both mobilization and immobilization from fear. As the therapist respects the autonomic state and holds the client in empathy and unconditional positive regard, the vagus nerve relaxes and brings the client into a calmer state.

Paying attention to a client's autonomic state and the accompanying defenses that present can be hard work. It involves respecting where the client is and recognizing that the client may be hesitant to let the clinician in. Clients may refuse to be vulnerable or to share emotional content. Large empathy invites the therapist to investigate what defenses and reactions to shame are occurring and to respect that the client is doing the best they can.

Defenses Against Shame

As illustrated by the shame hub in the introduction to this book, there are a variety of defenses against shame that a client may manifest, including blame, gaslighting, perfectionism, minimization, narcissistic self-inflation, rage, codependency, avoidance, hopelessness, addiction, and judgment. However, these are simply a few of the defenses against shame. It is important to always look deeper for indicators of shame, regardless of what the client brings to session. Over time, it gets easier to identify the signs of core shame in the therapy session, respecting how nonverbal clues, body posture, and movement all play a role.

Clients use *blame* as a defense mechanism when they point the finger at others and don't take responsibility for themselves. They may also assume a chronic victim role and feel that so much has been done to them that they can't possibly succeed. Oftentimes, blame goes hand in hand with *gaslighting*, in which someone doesn't respond with empathy to another's needs and instead minimizes the other person's experience and highlights their own problems. Looking at these defenses from the lens of shame-informed therapy, clinicians can see how clients project blame onto others in an attempt to minimize having to look at their own flaws. This type of projection is seen when individuals complain or criticize others. So many times, it becomes clear that the person projecting blame or gaslighting is truly hiding something they don't want others to see.

Perfectionism is another defense mechanism against shame that permeates Western culture today. Success is often viewed by how many accolades one achieves instead of how one feels about oneself on the inside. This need for perfectionism is particularly evident among high school students, where increased competition for college admissions has resulted in the need to get the "best grades" in order to get into the "best schools." Oftentimes, this type of overachievement behavior results in depression and anxiety.

Clients may also use *minimization* as a defense mechanism when they believe that their problems are not "big enough" to warrant therapy. They may refer to their difficulties as "first-world problems" and minimize their importance. We typically see this shame defense in clients who exhibit an avoidant attachment style, as they have learned to do everything on their own and don't necessarily ask for help.

In addition, *narcissistic self-inflation* is a defense that clients often use to hide feelings of inadequacy and failure that would be too painful to admit. These clients may brag about their accolades and appear as if they have it all together, when they are actually harboring the deep-seated feeling of being "not enough." Although people often mistake narcissism for too much self-love, it is actually a reflection of self-hatred.

Rage is another defense mechanism that reflects moving against shame. Anger gets intensified as the individual tries to defend themselves or convince someone else that they are right and that they need to get what they want. This dynamic sometimes presents in couples therapy. One partner is desperately trying to prove themselves right, but their shame keeps them in a state of dysregulation where they are unable to rationally or calmly negotiate their needs.

Although *codependency* is often not thought of as related to shame, this is a defense mechanism that protects clients against the belief that they are unlovable or unworthy. Clients who struggle with codependency are typically kind, generous, and always thinking about other people. However, they often provide this caregiving by sacrificing their own health and erecting poor boundaries. When clinicians look more closely and see this behavior as a defense against shame, it becomes clearer how over-giving is simply a way for clients to feel lovable and defend against shame.

When clients use *avoidance* as a defense mechanism, it reflects an example of moving away from shame. These clients avoid conflict at all costs and may isolate from others so as to not activate the core shame. *Hopelessness* is another type of moving away from shame that we often see with depression. Clients may exhibit the overwhelming feeling of never getting anywhere in life or having the things they desire. This type of defense can create a self-fulfilling prophecy that results in the continuation of the shame spiral.

Addiction represents another defense against shame that can come in many forms. Clients may turn to drugs, alcohol, work, food, sex, or other addictions to distract themselves from the feeling of "not enoughness." When clients don't want to look at the inner torment of shame, they easily choose a substance to numb it out. However, this results in an endless cycle of self-defeat and possibly self-destruction. Moreover, the shame that accompanies relapse only serves to reactivate the shame spiral.

Finally, *judgment* frequently occurs to offset core shame. Clients may criticize or ridicule others in an attempt to distract from their own feelings of inadequacy. In my own work, this type of defense mechanism frequently plays out among women who judge other women in the role of motherhood. Instead of supporting one another in a very important and demanding job, they are often critical and talk behind one another's backs. However, any sort of judgment can indicate shame.

Rewiring Neural Connections

Research shows us that the body holds on to the memories of trauma and shame and that these somatic memories often override cognitive thought processes (van der Kolk, 2014). This can result in a continued spiral of shame because the body's autonomic nervous system continues to respond to shame triggers, in turn overriding any cognitive thought processes that are attempting to counteract deeply engrained shame beliefs. Therefore, effective therapy for shame involves the use of top-down approaches, such as talk therapy and cognitive work, in combination with bottom-up approaches that viscerally contradict the trauma response (van der Kolk, 2014).

Part of this process involves working with clients to help them recognize what they are experiencing in their body when their left-brain narrative takes over. For example, clinicians can ask, "Where do you feel the anxiety in your body?" or "Are you experiencing anything physically when you think about the bullying?" At the same time, it is always important to keep in mind the subtle triggers that might occur in the therapeutic setting. Always use discretion and discernment when exploring body sensations. If someone has a history of sexual abuse for example, asking them to feel something in their body may be too much to ask.

Since core shame develops primarily in the nonverbal right brain, the goal of shame-informed therapy is to stimulate neuroplasticity and allow for the development of new neural networks associated with safety and connection (Cozolino, 2002). When a client has been relationally traumatized, the right-brain sense of self that develops is a "psychobiological, right-lateralized bodily-based process" (Shore, 2012, p. 296). It is made up of coping mechanisms and defenses that need to be overridden in the sensory body memory. Therefore, therapeutic experiences that promote safety and connection allow for the development of new neural pathways that were previously disconnected or pruned off. These new pathways help connect the damage from the early ruptures in the interpersonal bridges. Instead of reexperiencing feelings of shame and disintegration of self, the client experiences comfort and connection in the therapeutic setting, allowing new pathways to fire that promote healing in the brain.

Therefore, shame-informed therapy involves helping clients develop repeated interpersonal connections that feel safe, validating, and responsive so they can rewire the brain into a more authentic SELF. This process requires staying playful, curious, and accepting so clients can experience a new way of being in a relationship. **In particular, the shame-informed therapist works with clients to identify old patterns and begin to build more authentic relationships in therapy and outside of the session.** The therapist respects the old patterns that were set up early on and builds new networks of authenticity in the therapeutic relationship. An authentic relationship is:

- **A**ware of the feelings and behaviors that best reflect the present moment experience
- **U**ntethered in that it allows one to freely explore experiences instead of focusing on what one "should" do
- **T**ruthful and able to recognize what is true and speak it to others
- **H**opeful in recognizing that some things take time and that life is full of challenges

- **E**nergizing as one follows passions and desires congruent with the inborn essence of self
- **N**onjudgmental in realizing that everyone is on their own path and that there is no need to judge oneself or others
- **T**rustworthy because integrity lives in authentic relationships
- **I**ntrospective and willing to be quiet and look inward for answers
- **C**urious by always inquiring into situations for better understanding and relationships

Helping clients find more congruency in thought, feeling, and sensory experiences helps rewire the neural connections. Of course, building these new pathways takes time because rewiring neural connections requires sustained and consistent relational experiences (DeYoung, 2015). But over time and within the context of an empathetic therapeutic relationship, the disintegrated self begins to experience more cohesion as these neurons repeatedly fire and rewire into connection (DeYoung, 2015).

Since treating shame takes time and frequent experiences of attunement to rewire the sense of safety in the brain, it is easy for clients to fall back into old patterns, like feeling they are a failure, which reactivates the shame response. When this occurs, clinicians can use the analogy of a butterfly to bring hope into those moments of despair. In particular, before a butterfly emerges from its cocoon, it has imaginal cells that already know what it is going to

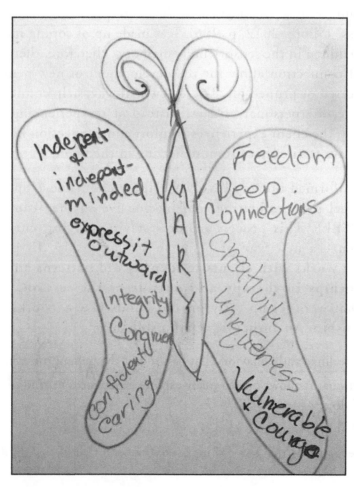

Figure 10. The Butterfly Effect

be. However, if the cocoon opens before the metamorphosis is complete, then the butterfly will die. This analogy can encourage clients to be patient with the process when it doesn't feel like they are where they want to be. They can list the qualities that describe their authentic self that are already there—waiting to emerge from the cocoon.

Figure 10 illustrates how I used this analogy with a client named Mary, who was frustrated that change wasn't happening fast enough in therapy. After describing the butterfly effect to her, she made a drawing of a butterfly and listed her authentic qualities on its wings. She kept this drawing as a reminder to herself that the inner work she was doing would eventually emerge more fully and that it was okay to be in the cocoon for now.

Exercises and Sample Re-Stories

The exercises in the next section can assist clients and clinicians with the process of respecting the autonomic response that gets activated in response to core shame. The **Do You Move Away, Toward, or Against?** worksheet asks clients to identify how they respond to stressful situations that activate shame, which can help them get in touch with their patterns of autonomic reactivity and the dysfunctional behavior patterns that ensue. The **Body Scan** worksheet helps clients pay attention to and identify what body sensations they experience when something activates their shame response.

The next two worksheets—**Old Story/New Story** and **The Spotlight Is on You!**—ask clients to write down what they notice about their old story and what they want to create instead as they re-story. **The Butterfly Effect** worksheet supports clients who feel like therapy is not progressing as quickly as they would like. Since it takes time to change deeply ingrained patterns, clients can also use the **My Three-Act Day: Affirm, Connect, and Trust** worksheet as a way to remember to practice bringing the affirmation into the body.

Finally, **The Art and Architecture of Reconstructing the Authentic SELF: RESPECTING the Autonomic State** worksheet asks clients to identify the defense mechanisms they may have used for emotional safety so they can better respect how these responses developed as a means to cope and survive.

Do You Move Away, Toward, or Against?

When we feel inadequate or not good enough in a situation, we tend to do one of three things: We either move away, move toward, or move against. Like a trauma response, the body reacts with fear. The frontal lobe then goes offline, making clear, rational thinking difficult. Recognizing your reaction is the first step in creating a more productive way to react.

The next time you are in a situation where you don't feel good enough, make a note of the situation and describe your reaction using this worksheet. Once you know your common "go-to" reactions, you can use the SAFE SELF worksheet from chapter 2 to find other ways to cope instead of reverting to the old patterns you've identified here.

Do you...

1. **Move away** (e.g., isolate, avoid, hide, keep secrets, withdraw)? If so, describe the situation and how it feels in your body.

   _____

   _____

   _____

   _____

   _____

   _____

2. **Move toward** (e.g., people pleasing, codependency, giving too much of yourself)? If so, describe the situation and how it feels in your body.

_____

_____

_____

_____

_____

3. **Move against** (e.g., lashing out, fighting back, hurting others, shaming others)? If so, describe the situation and how it feels in your body.

_____

_____

_____

_____

_____

Body Scan

Paying attention to where you feel sensations in your body can give you clues to where you might want to send extra self-compassion. The next time you are feeling inadequate or not good enough, use this worksheet to identify where you feel any tension in your body. Breathe into that area and imagine sending it some extra light and love.

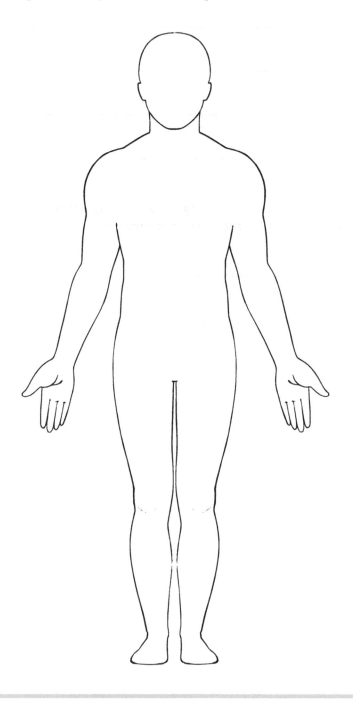

Old Story/New Story

It helps to recognize how we are changing our stories. In the box on the left, write down what is familiar to you, and in the box on the right, write down what you are creating that is different. For example, your old story may be "I'm overemotional just like my mother," and your new story may be "I am aware of my emotional self and express my feelings with kindness and respect."

My old story tells me:	My new story says:

The Spotlight Is on You!

Once you recognize old patterns of negative self-talk and self-defeating behavior, you can imagine something different that is healthier and more aligned with your authentic SAFE SELF. Imagine you are standing in the spotlight of an old belief, such as "I have to sacrifice so I can take care of everyone else." Write that in the first circle.

Then, change the story to something else, such as "It's important to take care of my own needs before I help others." Write that new story in the second circle. If you prefer, you can draw images that represent the old and the new. Then, close your eyes and imagine yourself stepping out of one spotlight into the other. You can even draw two large circles on the floor representing the old belief and the new belief. Step out of the old story into the new and feel what it's like to take on a new YOU!

Old negative self-talk and self-defeating behavior

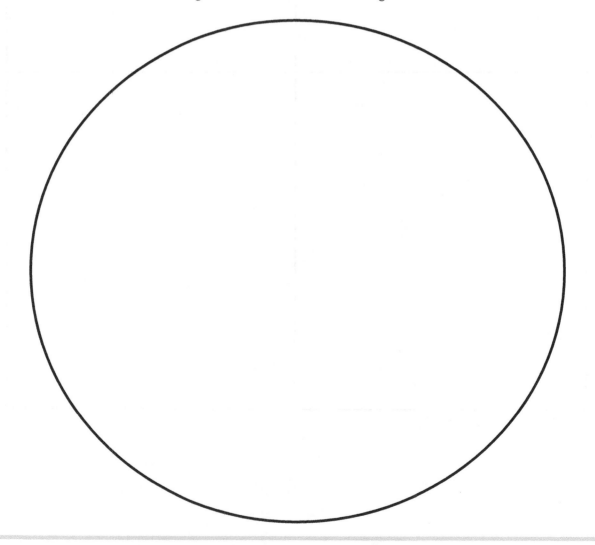

The Spotlight Is on You!

Your new authentic SAFE SELF

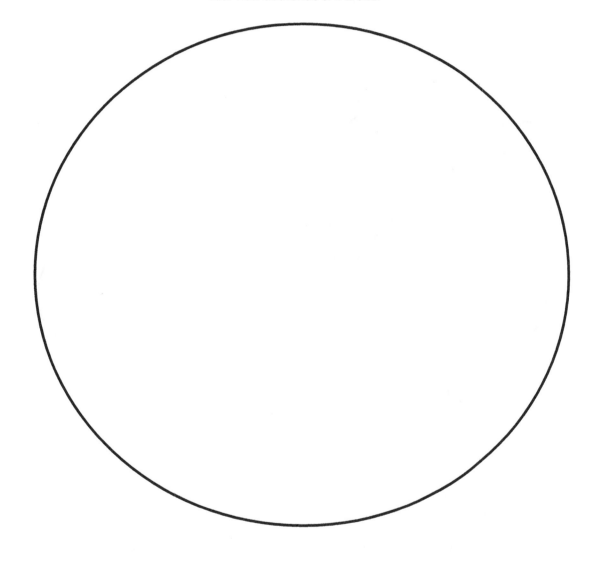

The Butterfly Effect

When a butterfly is in its cocoon, it has imaginal cells that know exactly what it will transform into. But if the butterfly emerges from its cocoon too soon, then it will die. Sometimes, it is hard to wait for transformations in ourselves. To help you stay patient with the process, it can help to remember the qualities of your authentic self that already exist within you but are waiting to emerge. Write down adjectives that describe your authentic self in the wings of this butterfly.

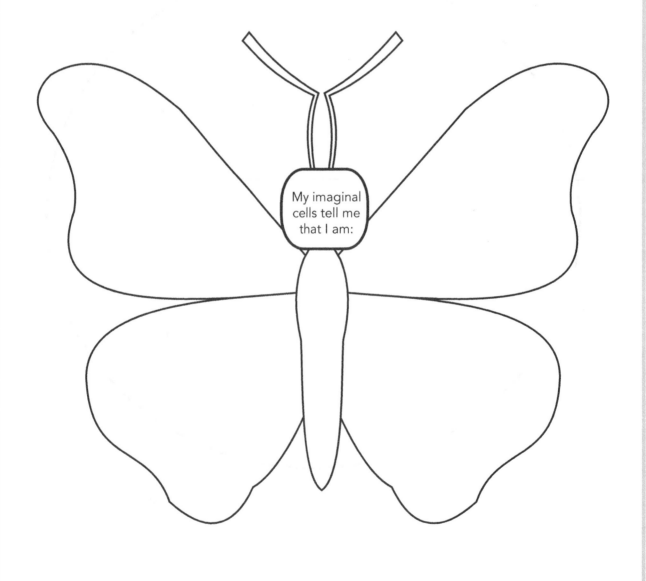

My imaginal cells tell me that I am:

My Three-Act Day: Affirm, Connect, and Trust

Changing old patterns and self-defeating behaviors requires repetition and reminders. For example, perhaps you are working on affirming the story that you are lovable. Use this worksheet as a daily reminder to *affirm* your new storyline, *connect* to how it feels in your body, and *trust* that over time your body memory will become familiar with the new story and develop it as truth. Do this first thing in the morning, midday, and before you go to bed each night for at least a week. Check each box when you have completed it.

My 3 Acts:	AM Affirmation	AM Connect	AM Trust	Noon Affirmation	Noon Connect	Noon Trust	PM Affirmation	PM Connect	PM Trust
Monday									
Tuesday									
Wednesday									
Thursday									
Friday									
Saturday									
Sunday									

Write your affirmation here: _____

_____

Reconstructing the Authentic SELF:
RESPECTING the Autonomic State
(Wiring, Plumbing, Closets, and Cabinets)

When you feel judged, unheard, or unseen, it is not uncommon to lash out, blame others, or engage in a variety of other coping responses. You can respect these responses by thinking of them as survival defenses that you used to find emotional safety.

You can liken these safety behaviors to the *wiring* that runs through the house, with your flow of awareness regarding these behaviors as the *plumbing*. Using the house template, identify the types of defense mechanisms you use when you aren't able to express your feelings versus how you react when you are able to express yourself. Then, think of any secrets you might be hiding in the *closets and cabinets,* and who might be a safe person to tell them to.

Before you complete the house worksheet, here are two thought questions you can write about.

When I wasn't able to express my emotions today, here is what happened:

_____

_____

When I was able to express my emotions today, here is what happened:

_____

_____

Reconstructing the Authentic Self
RESPECTING the Autonomic State
(Wiring, Plumbing, Closets, and Cabinets)

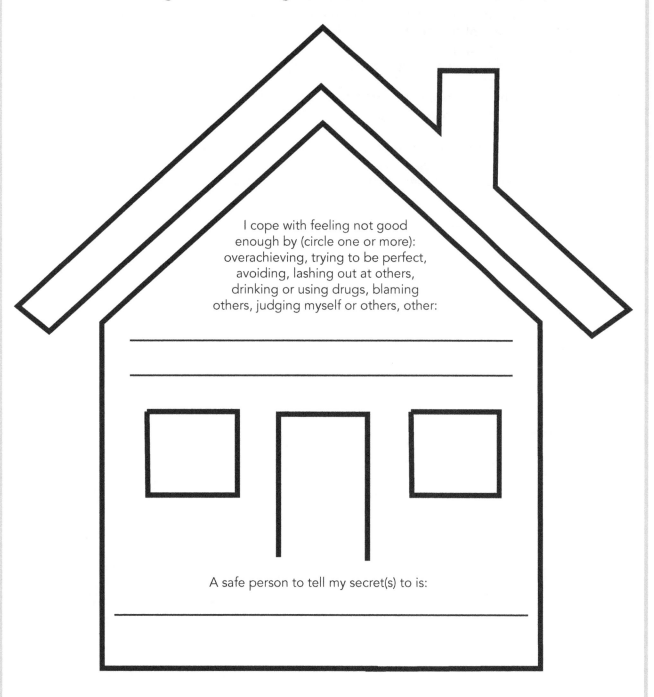

I cope with feeling not good enough by (circle one or more): overachieving, trying to be perfect, avoiding, lashing out at others, drinking or using drugs, blaming others, judging myself or others, other:

A safe person to tell my secret(s) to is:

Sample Re-Story: The Spotlight Is on You! (Sharon)

Sharon was a mother of three teenagers who had moved from the East Coast to Colorado for her husband's job. She didn't want to move, and it was a difficult transition for her and her children. Shortly after they moved, she discovered her husband was having an affair and drinking heavily. They did some work in couples counseling and he got sober. However, Sharon had exhibited a pattern of codependency most of her life. She always had to take care of her mother, even as a child. Her mother recently died, and Sharon was grieving and working with ways to better take care of herself. She had a hard time standing up for her own needs given her history of sacrifice.

To embody the idea of something different, I suggested she use the spotlight exercise to imagine stepping out of her current story of codependency into a new story of self-care.

Old Story: I have to sacrifice so I can take care of everyone else.

Re-Story: It's important to take care of my own needs before I help others.

7

REGULATE in the Dance of Co-Regulation

"Shame is paralyzing and debilitating. It invites us not to be heard, at least not in an authentic way. Acting courageously when shame enters the picture requires extraordinary courage because people will do anything to escape from shame or from the possibility that shame will be evoked. It is just too difficult to go there. Even for people who will walk into the fires of transformation to face fear."

—Dr. Harriet Lerner

Safe Emergency

Therapy is a place of "safe emergency" in which clients learn to confront challenges and stressors in the context of a supportive interpersonal environment. In the safety of the therapy room, clients can move from anxiety and depression into curiosity and exploration (Cozolino, 2002). The clinician's major role is to help clients feel safe in the world and in their own skin. A safe emergency challenges growth and helps clients integrate new experiences of support and guidance.

The safe emergency is the place where the client and clinician dance together to co-regulate and enhance cortical functioning related to the stories that activate core shame. The therapist is similar to a surrogate good enough parent, modeling the regulatory abilities of the social brain. Over time, the client internalizes these skills and sculpts new neural structures for regulating emotions. As clients learn to expect relief from disconnection in the therapeutic setting, which is in contrast to their earlier unrepaired ruptures, they develop a sense of safety and increase their ability to tolerate the intensity of shame-based feelings.

For clients to let go of the past, they have to process past experiences within their window of tolerance (Siegel, 1999). The window of tolerance refers to the optimal state of arousal where cortical functioning stays intact. In this state, clients can absorb and process information more effectively. When the client is outside this optimal zone, the prefrontal cortex shuts down, resulting in a decrease in cognitive processing and an increase in sensorimotor responses (Siegel, 1999). For example, if clients are in a state of hyperarousal, they might experience increased tension, disorganized thoughts, emotional reactivity, and intrusive imagery. And if they are in a state of hypoarousal, they may experience emotional numbing, reduced physical movement, absence of sensation, or minimal cognitive processing. It is also possible for both dysregulated states to occur simultaneously, which we can compare to driving a car with both the accelerator and the brakes at the same time.

We can relate the window of tolerance back to the polyvagal theory in that hypoarousal reflects dorsal vagal activation (decelerating the body by slowing down heart rate and breathing to conserve energy), whereas hyperarousal reflects a sympathetic state of mobilization (accelerating the body into fight-or-flight). In contrast, the social engagement system of the vagus nerve helps clients to put on the "brakes" and to work within their window of tolerance. When we work with trauma and shame in psychotherapy, we are often in a dance of co-regulation, noticing when clients may be moving in and out of their window of tolerance and helping them to find the vagal "brake" that slows the car down.

Co-Regulating Safety and Equal Power

Early interactive experiences determine how well an individual can utilize the therapeutic relationship. Even when clients are longing for trusting relationships, they still live with irrational fears that can interfere with their ability to self-regulate in therapy (Herman, 2007). To remain connected to and tolerate a client's dysregulated shame states, it is important for therapists to work with their own shame proneness. This is because co-regulating with clients into a ventral vagal state of social engagement is an interpersonal right-brain activity. Attuned right-brain therapy gives both the client and the therapist ongoing opportunities for a better connection with themselves and others. Noticing the nonverbal clues to shame happens more efficiently when the clinician has fine-tuned skills of right-brain regulation.

Given that co-regulation is a right-brain process, clients who come to session feeling inadequate and flawed can activate the clinician's right-brain mirror neurons, and the feeling of not being a good enough therapist might emerge. Maintaining a keen awareness of this countertransference allows the clinician to return to a ventral vagal state of calm by activating an awareness of being a good enough therapist. This self-regulated affect is then reflected in the client's mirror neurons, and both client and clinician return to a calmer emotional state.

This is the dance. *Co-regulating* is an ongoing process of feeling into the relationship and developing healthy attunement skills knowing that mirror neurons can activate feelings for the clinician that may not be their own. Assessing and co-regulating right-brain material is an interpersonal process that witnesses a client's values without imposing one's own, balances power so as not to be the expert, and affirms strengths. Clinicians who cannot tolerate their own shame will easily get dysregulated when the client's shame defenses appear. If any doubts about being a good enough therapist emerge in session, shame-prone clients will sense that affect. Supervision and self-analysis are important to supporting the ongoing co-regulation process when working with shame-informed therapy.

The dance of co-regulation demands full attention and presence from therapists as they merge with right-brain affect. To stay present and regulated during this process, therapists may find it helpful to imagine their right brain seeing and feeling the client's right brain while visualizing a figure eight of the flow between them (Figure 11).

Figure 11. Sustaining Right-Brain Co-Regulation

Being present with the client's defenses against shame without trying to fix them is key. Recognizing and respecting the coping mechanisms that are in place, even when it is uncomfortable for the clinician, helps both parties regulate emotional content. Clients need to feel sustained empathy without any advice. This may seem counterintuitive to the role of clinician, especially in the world of managed healthcare that demands fast solution-focused therapies. However, giving up the role of the expert and stepping into the client's experience with empathy is necessary to heal shame. Right-brain healing is nonverbal, so being with the client and holding a safe emotional space is more important than trying to impose a therapeutic technique looking for results.

Another important step in the process of co-regulating is establishing equal power (Figure 12). Sometimes, clients put clinicians on a pedestal. The therapist can remedy this by being personable, playful, and curious, which tames the common core shame feeling of being exposed as flawed. For example, being personable helps build a more relaxed interaction where there is less differentiation between therapist and client. In addition, being playful—as opposed to rigidly adhering to therapeutic techniques—invites clients to be open to spontaneity. Finally, exhibiting an attitude of curiosity invites exploration and unconditional positive regard. Asking questions without judgment helps clients feel connected.

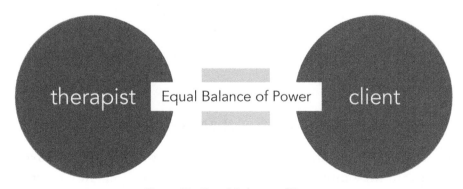

Figure 12. Equal Balance of Power

Sometimes, therapists activate their own shame when progress in therapy is slow. They begin to wonder what they are doing wrong and how they might provide different interventions to move clients past a stuck point. Meeting clients where they are without expectation or judgment creates a safe environment of unconditional acceptance, one that may have been missing in childhood, and is very therapeutic in terms of rewiring neural networks. When the clinician can stay patient with the process and the frequent repetition of old narratives, it models self-acceptance.

Ultimately, the process of co-regulating with a client into a ventral vagal state requires integrating right-brain sensory information with the left-brain thinking process, all while holding awareness of the autonomic state. The goal is to help the client feel a sense of safety and regulate into a ventral vagal state of social engagement (Figure 13).

The sections that follow provide some right-brain sensory activities that can help clients regulate into a ventral vagal state. These exercises involve creative arts, poetry, and other body-centered techniques to co-regulate and re-story the core shame memories. Clinicians can also use the **Personal Interest Inventory** (chapter 3) to access what type of creative expression clients might be willing to use in session or as homework. Finding out a client's likes and dislikes is useful so clinicians can suggest an appropriate sensory modality that embodies the cognitive material that has emerged.

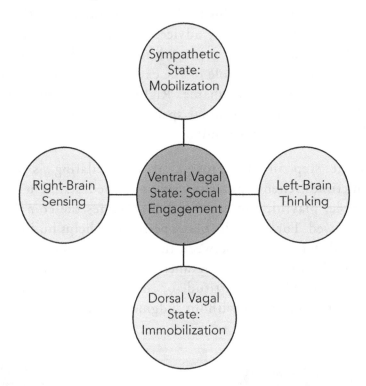

Figure 13. Co-Regulating into a Ventral Vagal State

Creative Arts and Mandala Drawing

Gaining access to the right brain through creative arts helps clients move out of their logical left brain and into the sensory healing of creative expression. In particular, creative arts can help the right brain develop new neural connections with an experience that was previously unknown or inaccessible. It also shuts down some of the repetitive thoughts in the left brain and enables clients to relax into a regulated state of calm.

However, some clients are resistant to creative expression because they may have been shamed as children and told they were not good enough at art. Although it is important to never pressure a client into an activity that doesn't feel comfortable to them, adult coloring books can be a good way to introduce clients to art even if there is resistance. They give clients easy access to a process of simply adding color to the page.

Collages and vision boards are also great creative art exercises. Clients can glue pictures, images, words, stickers, and scrapbooking items to a poster board representing what they envision for a new narrative. Some clients may prefer other types of creative arts expression, such as drawing, painting, sculpting, woodworking, or others. Clinicians may have some of these materials available in office, or they can suggest clients create with their preferred medium at home.

A mandala (which is Sanskrit for "sacred circle") is another form of creative expression in which clients simply draw a circle and then freely express whatever emerges. Carl Jung adopted this technique in describing the circle drawings that he invited his clients to create. Jung associated the mandala with the center of the personality, describing how this center has an irresistible compulsion to become what it truly is (Jung, 1963): the authentic self.

Circles appear in nature in the sun, the moon, and the earth. They have also been seen throughout history in ancient rock carvings, Native American sand drawings, Tibetan mandalas, and stained-glass windows in cathedrals. We can think of mandalas as *telescopes into the soul*, giving clients glimpses into what their true longings and desires are through symbolic representations. Creating mandalas is a meditative, healing activity that brings to light expressions of the authentic self.

If clients require more structure to get started on a mandala drawing, the methods described by Heussenstamm (2016) and Fincher (1991) can provide this needed structure. For example, clients can divide their circle into eight sections and in each section draw images that have emerged in a guided meditation. Clients may also prefer to do this on black paper to represent their unconscious mind. Clients can do this activity individually or in groups. Individual sessions take longer than an hour, so the client can start the mandala drawing process in session and complete it at home or over several sessions. Clinicians may find that using mandalas

Figure 14. Mandala Drawing

in session can be particularly helpful with adolescents, who tend to get a bit uncomfortable simply sitting and talking. Figure 14 portrays a mandala created by a fifteen-year-old client with major anxiety, which she drew over the course of a four-week span.

Prosody in Music and Poetry

Prosody, which is the rhythm under words and is most commonly noticed in music and poetry, is the most significant form of sensory healing (Porges, 2011). However, how we respond to sounds varies as a function of pitch, as mammals have sound-perception abilities that allow them to distinguish safety cues based on frequency. Low-frequency monotone sounds, such as a dog barking and thunder, as well as high-frequency monotone sounds, such as a baby's cry or a scream, are signals of danger. To cue safety, soothing sounds within the frequencies of social communication, such as lullabies, soft music, and soothing nature sounds, are helpful. Providing soft, soothing music either on its own or with guided meditation is a great therapeutic tool.

Every client is different, so it helps to know the type of sound they resonate with. Music provides many opportunities for prosody and healing in the right brain. Sometimes, clients share a song and it informs a new narrative, regulates emotion, and provides a sensory reminder of the re-story between sessions. When appropriate, clinicians can use the session as an opportunity to listen to the songs clients have mentioned because doing so can activate several aspects of social engagement by balancing power, facilitating empathy, drawing on the power of prosody, and building the therapeutic relationship.

Another way to work with music is to find a brave song that clients can play when they are feeling scared or a calm song they can play when they are stressed. You can also use Tibetan singing bowls at the beginning of a group or during session to set a tone of mindfulness and presence. Other sound-healing opportunities that might appeal to clients include drumming circles, kirtan chanting, and gong baths.

Some clients may be musicians who already use this medium as a form of healing. For example, I had a new client recently say he liked to write songs and play the guitar, but because of his perfectionism and anxiety, it was stressful for him at times. I suggested he play just for fun and let go of needing to win an award, allowing the music to help him relax.

Poetry is another way you can bring prosody into the session, given that the prosodic melody of poetry is within the frequencies of social engagement and cues safety. A few poems that clinicians may find helpful in the treatment of core shame are "Unfold Your Own Myth" by Rumi, "Joy and Sorrow" by Kahlil Gibran, "The Summer Day" by Mary Oliver, and "The Guest House" by Rumi. If there is a poem that resonates with a client's story, it may be therapeutic to read it aloud to them and then give them a copy they can reference later. Clients may also want to write their own poetry, using either free verse, haiku, or other methods. Sharing what they wrote, if they so desire, is a wonderful social engagement tool as well.

Movement and Ritual

Helping clients connect to what is happening in their body is an important part of shame work. Clients may have a history of dissociation and collapse, or they may intellectualize the story as a coping mechanism. By incorporating movement and other rituals into their daily routine, clients can enhance the body memory and activate feelings of being good enough. When clients pay attention to how their body moves throughout the day, it brings awareness to how powerful the body memory is. For instance, I recently moved my psychotherapy office, and even though I confirmed the new address with clients on the day of their session, several of them still went to the old office. This example illustrates how the body memory often takes over cognitive thought, which helps clients understand why thinking may not be the solution to their problems.

Once you know the type of activities your client is interested in, you can suggest taking the core shame theme you are working on and translating it into a movement experience the client enjoys, even if it is simply taking a walk. Yoga, dance, and martial arts are some movement practices clients might already enjoy. Yoga in particular increases heart rate variability and improves blood flow to the heart. Nia is another form of movement that uses a combination of yoga, dance, and martial arts to integrate mind, body, and emotions. It was created as a way to feel joy in movement (Rosas & Rosas, 2005).

In addition, daily rituals, such as morning or evening meditation practices, can provide clients with a rhythm that supports the nervous system in staying calm. For example, they can possibly start the day by reading from an inspirational daily meditation book, journaling about their dreams, or doing a guided meditation. Their evening ritual may look similar but also include the addition of a gratitude practice. By writing down everything they are grateful for that day, clients remind themselves that even when there is stress, there are other experiences of joy around them as well. Other rituals can include burning whatever it is a client wants to release into a fire, or washing their hands and feet to represent cleansing away the old in order to be fresh for the new. Anything that provides a sensory experience toward a new story is helpful in rewiring the brain.

Clients can also schedule mindfulness moments throughout the day, which remind them to take a deep breath and reground themselves as a means of calming the nervous system. Slowing down the exhale and extending it for two to four seconds longer than usual activates the parasympathetic system, which increases the vagal influence and releases any anxiety and tension in the body. As clients exhale, they can imagine a warm healing elixir coming from the base of their skull running down through the vagus nerve and all around into their body.

Clinicians can also invite clients to do some body stances in session that somatically address their reactions to shame. For example, they can embody staying in courage by standing with their knees bent, their feet hip-width apart, and their arms stretched out and bent at the elbows, pointing upward, similar to a martial arts sumo stance. They can also develop love for themselves and others as they physically scoop love in with their hands by reaching out with their arms and pulling their hands toward their heart. And they can let go of negative self-talk and fear by wiggling and shaking their body as a means of releasing it (Hendricks & Hendricks, 2016). Stanley Rosenberg's *Accessing the Healing Power of the Vagus Nerve* (2017) provides other suggestions for body-centered practices for healing the vagal nerve.

Playfulness and Humor

In today's society, where staying busy and being productive is the expectation, adults are actively discouraged from taking time to rest and play (Brown, 2010b). To them, taking time to play may be considered lazy or unproductive. But the reality is that play can improve health and facilitate present-moment awareness. When adults engage in an activity for enjoyment and recreation, it can help rewire the brain by shifting the logical mind back into the imagination, which can then engage curiosity and compassion. Simply put, play provides rest and rejuvenation, and it shapes the brain by fostering joy, creativity, and innovation (Brown, 2010b).

Since clients may not set aside time for play, modeling a playful stance in therapy by bringing humor and lightness into the session gives clients an opportunity to *feel into* the right-brain experience of pleasure and fun. Playfulness in the therapy room also helps repair earlier attachment ruptures caused by caregiver-child interactions that did not foster interpersonal synchrony.

One playful tool that clinicians can use with clients is the image of a *Nuff* (Figure 15). This idea emerged one week in group supervision when I was talking about my research on core shame and the notion that "I am enough." In response, one of the psychologists in the group jokingly said, "You're a Nuff. I didn't know you were from Nuff!" The idea resonated so much that I asked a friend to draw an image of a Nuff. Over time, the Nuff has become a useful

Figure 15. "I am a Nuff." Drawing by Laura Martinez.

therapeutic intervention that brings playfulness, laughter, and lightness to the session—with clients of all ages. After showing clients an image of the Nuff and asking how they feel in their body, they often acknowledge a feeling of lightness, playfulness, and relaxation. It reminds clients that these are the feelings we want to develop to create more of those neural pathways in the brain.

Nature and Animals

Nature is another tremendous healer that can provide the sensory and meditative experiences needed to help clients regulate into a ventral vagal state. Simply taking a walk or sitting under a tree while observing the beauty of their surroundings, listening to nature's sounds, and smelling the scents can be healing. These mindful nature experiences offer those quiet moments that help to rewire safety in the brain. Touching a tree or smelling a flower is a simple way to bring pleasure and safety into experiences. Rocks and shells and other pieces of earth can also be grounding for clients. In addition, observing how nature grows and changes slowly over time is a great metaphor for clients who feel like therapy is not progressing fast enough.

Finally, animals can be tremendously healing, both as domesticated pets and symbolic representations. Pets love unconditionally and often provide clients with feelings of connection and appreciation, which can be a helpful way to visualize those feelings in the body. Sometimes, though, even an animal that has a fleeting presence in a client's life may have deeper meaning. For example, a client came in one day after having to stop on the road because a deer was crossing. Upon looking up the symbolism for deer in *Animal Speak*—a comprehensive dictionary of animal symbolism by Ted Andrews (2002)—it became clear that the deer represented many of the qualities the client wanted to embody, including gentleness, innocence, and clear vision. To use animal symbolism with clients, clinicians may find it useful to have bowls filled with animal cards in their office. Clients love the hands-on aspect of the cards, as well as the symbolic meaning relevant to them that they can work on throughout the next week or even longer.

Exercises and Sample Re-Stories

On the pages that follow, there are several exercises and worksheets that clinicians can use with clients to help them regulate into a ventral vagal state. However, use discretion and keen sensing when suggesting worksheets and exercises, as offering too many activities can portray the therapist as the expert, in turn disrupting the balance of power needed to co-regulate. When the time feels appropriate to present a worksheet or exercise, do so without it feeling too clinical and shaming.

You can use the **Mandala of Love and Belonging** worksheet as a template for creating a mandala drawing. Prior to starting the drawing, clients may wish to reference the **I Am Enough Meditation** (chapter 2) to connect to the subconscious experience of love and belonging and to access some images for the mandala drawing. For clients who would benefit from more structure, you can use **Mandala Drawing with Stencils** to explain the group or individual process of drawing mandalas using stencils and black paper.

The next two exercises focus on the healing power of prosody through the use of poetry and sound. In particular, clients can use the **Healing Haiku** to create their own poems and give voice to the nonverbal aspects of themselves. They can also use the **Find Your Brave Song** worksheet to identify a song that gives them courage, using the worksheet as a reminder to play the song whenever they need to feel strong.

The **Bowls of Light Ritual** is another form of creative expression that can remind clients to find their inner light. It is based on the Hawaiian fairy tale from *Tales from the Night Rainbow* (Willis & Lee, 1990). The grandmother in the story tells a little boy about how everyone is born with a perfect bowl of light, which over time gets covered up with struggles, trauma, and pain. But the truth is, all we need to do is turn the bowl over. The light is always there.

Finally, **The Art and Architecture of Reconstructing the Authentic SELF: REGULATING the Autonomic State** worksheet asks clients to identify any barriers that might be getting in the way of relational presence and the dance of co-regulation, as well as what might be hiding in the unconscious mind.

Mandala of Love and Belonging

The act of coloring a mandala can be calming, as it activates the right brain and gives the logical mind and nervous system a brief respite. Without thinking too much, draw whatever shapes and colors feel like love and belonging to you in the circle. As you color, replace any worry thoughts that arise with thoughts of love and belonging, such as "I am loved, and I belong." Don't worry about whether or not your mandala is good "art." Simply let go into the experience. You can also write about this experience later in your journal, if you choose.

Mandala Drawing with Stencils

Creating a mandala is a meditative, healing activity that brings expressions of the authentic self into the light. In this activity, you'll use black paper to represent your unconscious mind, and you'll have an opportunity to use stencils to convey any thoughts or images that you want to bring to light.

Materials Needed:

- Black paper cut into 12 × 12 inch squares

- White and colored pencils

- Gel pens and markers

- Electric pencil sharpener

- Various stencils

- Ruler

- Protractor and a compass (or plate) to draw a large circle

Directions:

1. Prior to creating your mandala, listen to a guided relaxation meditation to help calm your body and mind. When you are finished, jot down any shapes, colors, or images that emerged for you during the meditation.

2. Then, draw a circle on a piece of black paper and divide it into eight equal parts using a white pencil. To decorate your mandala, choose any stencils that represent the images elicited by the meditation.

3. Place the images around the circle in whatever way feels right. For example, you may place the image in each of the eight sections, in the center, or in only four sections. However you decide to place the images is up to you. This is a creative process. There is no right or wrong.

4. After you've drawn all your chosen images around the circle with a white pencil, use colored pencils, pens, or markers to fill in the images.

5. Once your mandala is complete, you have a *telescope into the soul* that can serve as a reminder of the soul's desires. You can find an example of what a completed mandala might look like on the next page, but remember that everyone's mandala will look different. Yours will be unique to you.

Sample Mandala Drawing

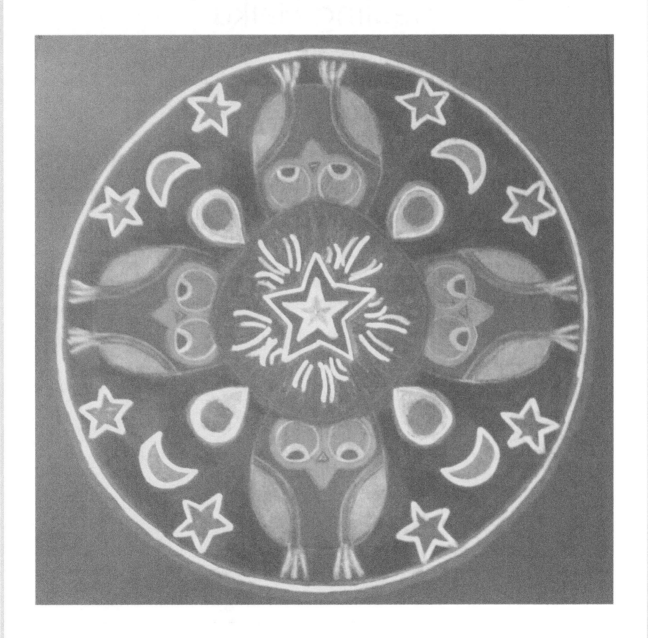

Healing Haiku

Poetry helps us give voice to what is sometimes nonverbal, bridging the right and left hemispheres of the brain. Some people simply start writing, letting the words flow into a poem, while other people need more of a format to bring their words to life. One suggested format is a Japanese haiku, which is a verse in three lines:

Line one has 5 syllables.

Line two has 7 syllables.

Line three has 5 syllables.

Here are some examples of haikus:

Shame in my body Feels like I can't breathe or move. What am I to do?	Empathy in me Allows me to see your truth. Let me look at you.
Courage within me Makes me strong and holds me up. I am safe with me.	Love in my body Feels so scary and locked up. Can I open up?

If you are ready, try out this poetry exercise by writing a haiku or any other type of poem that speaks to you. First, take a deep breath and feel your body. Then, see if you can name a feeling in your body and describe it with a poem. Don't worry about how "good" your poem is. Simply write and let the words flow.

_____

_____

_____

_____

_____

Find Your Brave Song

What song helps you feel strong? _____

_____

What is it about the song that inspires you? _____

_____

_____

What are some of the lyrics to the song that give you courage? _____

_____

_____

Listen to this song when you need courage!

Bowls of Light Ritual

In their book *Tales from the Night Rainbow*, Pali Jae Lee and Koko Willis tell us the following ancient Hawaiian story of the bowls of light:

Everyone is born with a bowl of perfect light. When taught to respect and love the light, we will grow in strength and health and can swim with the sharks, fly with the birds, and know and understand all things. When we are in fear, worry, doubt, judgment, anger, resentment, envy, or jealousy, some of the light will go out because these troubles add stones into the bowl of light, and light and stone cannot occupy the same space. If we continue to get stones in the bowl, the light will eventually go out, and just like a stone, we will no longer grow, or be capable of movement. However, all that is needed to release these feelings is to turn the bowl upside down and let the stones fall out. The light can then shine again and grow even brighter than before.

You can use this ritual in weekend retreats or across the course of two psychotherapy sessions. To complete the activity, you will need fast-drying clay, hand wipes, permanent markers, acrylic paint, paintbrushes, small stones, and votive candles.

The first part of the ritual is to have clients create a clay bowl that will dry overnight. Allow clients to shape and create a bowl that they will use for the ritual. The sensory aspects of this exercise are interesting to observe. Some clients don't like the feel of the clay and the messiness of the exercise. Guide clients through this discomfort by providing hand wipes and encouragement.

Although getting into the body is important in this process, if a client is too uncomfortable, this may not be appropriate just yet.

If there is time, clients may want to paint the bowl with acrylic paints, or they can leave it the natural color that it is. After completing the bowl, place a votive candle inside of it and play or sing a chant about light or self-love.

The second part of the ritual can take place at the next session or the following day if used during a weekend retreat. Invite clients to write words that represent what is coming up for them, such as *fear, anger, resentment, jealously,* or *grief,* on each of the stones. They can place the stones in the bowl throughout the session, and at the end, they can give the stones back to the earth (represented by a basket in the center of the room). Then, relight the candle in a closing song.

Once clients are finished with the ritual, invite them to write their impressions and feelings regarding the bowls of light activity in their journal.

Reconstructing the Authentic Self
REGULATING with the Client
(Lighting and Fences)

Oftentimes, you may not be aware of the reasons why you behave a certain way. Old, unconscious patterns that were set up when you were very young often create reactions that are not productive. These behaviors were the only way you knew how to feel emotionally safe in certain situations. You may also have learned to put up barriers to relationships because you are afraid of being hurt. Using this worksheet as a guide, think about the *lighting* in your house as a tool to see what might be hiding in the dark, and think about how the *fences* around your house may interfere with relational presence.

Today I noticed I have been hiding this part of myself:

_____

_____

_____

Sample Re-Story: Art (Karen)

Karen was raised by critical parents and felt like she was never good enough in their eyes. For example, her father had wanted a boy, so he refused to allow Karen to watch sports with him because she was a girl. Her mother frequently insulted her by telling her she was ugly or fat. Her mother also told her she wasn't a very good artist. In therapy, Karen was sometimes frustrated by her slow process of healing. We used the image of a tree to represent how she was actually growing and changing even though it was slow and sometimes difficult to see. She shared how she always loved to draw trees but didn't think she was good enough. I suggested she draw them anyway and let go of whether they were good.

Since Karen had two small children and a busy life, drawing with a pen and a sketch pad was something she could do anytime she had a few extra minutes. When she showed me some of her drawings, I was impressed by her skill level and encouraged her to keep drawing. Months later, she printed these images and created greeting cards for her friends and family. Her mother commented that "there weren't any leaves" on the tree, but Karen was able to recognize this negative message and re-story into the knowing that her trees were enough. And even more than enough, they were her design and beautiful just the way they were.

Old Story: I am not good enough to do art.

Re-Story: I enjoy doing art, and I am good enough.

Sample Re-Story: I Am a Nuff (Kelly)

Kelly was a sixteen-year-old girl who reported feeling "not smart enough" after taking the PSAT and getting a lower score than some of her peers. She also didn't earn as many A's during the semester as she usually did and was worried about her ability to get into medical school in a few years. When I asked her to describe the feeling in her body when she didn't feel smart enough, she reported feeling it in her throat and her solar plexus. She had internalized these events into a core belief about herself that said she was not good enough.

We talked about separating the *deed* from the *doer* and recognizing that she was doing the best she could. I suggested she breathe into her throat and her solar plexus and experience self-love. I then gave her a postcard with the picture of a Nuff and told her to use that image to remember that she was enough. She smiled, feeling much better about herself, and said she was going to make an "enough jar" where she could write suggested ways to love herself. She pasted the picture of the Nuff on the jar and called it her "Nuff Jar."

Old Story: I am not good enough.

Re-Story: I am enough.

Sample Re-Story: Prosody (Cory)

Cory was a fifteen-year-old male who came to see me after a failed suicide attempt and hospitalization. He had witnessed his father sexually assaulting a babysitter a few years before and later revealed he himself had been sexually assaulted by a man parked in a van in his neighborhood. He was depressed and highly anxious, but he still maintained honor-roll status at his magnet school. He liked to play the piano and guitar and would often do so in the evenings as a way to process his emotions. At the end of his junior year, he came out as gay.

After working in therapy for a few years and revealing his deeply hidden secrets, he rewrote a new narrative of self-love and acceptance. He also started writing poetry and published his first book right after high school graduation. Here is a line from one of his poems: "I am no Buddha, no Jesus, but a man seeking secrets in the feathers of a dove."

Old Story: I am ashamed of myself and my secrets.

Re-Story: I am not responsible for other people's actions, and I am lovable.

RE-STORY an Authentic Safe Experience of Living Freely (SELF)

"Each entered the forest at a point that he himself had chosen, where it was darkest and there was no way or no path. If there is a path, it is someone else's path and you are not on the adventure."

—Joseph Campbell

Connecting the Dots to Core Shame

In shame-informed therapy, the clinician is continually searching for clues in affect and behavior that help connect the dots to core shame so clients can re-story their authentic self. In particular, re-storying is a multilayered process that starts by connecting the dots from the client's current feelings to earlier experiences that may have set up neural pathways related to shame. The therapist works with the right-brain regulation by mirroring the client's feelings and helping the client to come into greater body awareness and somatic expression. This process gives shame back to its origin. The client learns it isn't about who they are but, rather, what happened to them.

The process of connecting the dots is best illustrated by John, who initially came to therapy for help in setting boundaries with his family of origin. He had recently sent a letter to his family requesting that they limit their visits. The response he subsequently received from his family was very shaming, as his mother and sister accused him of being selfish and not caring about the family.

When John first came to therapy, he only knew that he was angry about the letter from his family. However, by using the **Excavation Exercise** from chapter 2, John was able to uncover deeper feelings and realize that he actually felt unaccepted. This realization opened a door into his earlier experiences of feeling unaccepted that lived in his sensory memory. For example, on a somatic level, John reported that this feeling of being unaccepted was associated with tightness in his chest. When asked to connect that sensation to an earlier memory when he experienced a similar feeling, he described being teased for stuttering while growing up. John had been a severe stutterer since early childhood. He was often told to stop stuttering and was shamed for his awkward speech. He was bullied at school and sent away to a stuttering camp each summer. The experience of receiving the letter from his family unearthed the same feeling of shame that he had experienced while being teased as a child.

In further discussing his feeling of being unaccepted, as well as the similar feeling he experienced during childhood, it became clear that John's feeling of being unaccepted had actually become an overall feeling of being unacceptable. Core shame had become part of his identity rather than being isolated to a one-time incident. The events of his childhood had led him to the core belief that he was unacceptable. Throughout this process of connecting the dots, John was able to identify this underlying core shame belief even though the word *shame* had not been used yet in his treatment.

After working to counteract his shame belief, John identified a new sense of authentic truth by telling himself, "I am acceptable just the way I am." To help him re-story his sense of self, he repeated this affirmation to himself daily. He also embodied this new story while he showered, allowing the water to run over him and cleanse his old belief of not being acceptable. Figure 16 illustrates the process of connecting the dots in John's story.

Clinicians can also help clients connect the dots by educating them on the four therapeutic R's. For instance, when a client says, "I don't know why I can't think clearly when I'm angry" or "I don't know why it's so hard for me to change this pattern," it can be helpful to explain Porges's polyvagal theory. Doing so helps demystify the feeling of being emotionally stuck and allows clients to better understand their old story, which then paves the way for them to recognize, respect, regulate, and re-story.

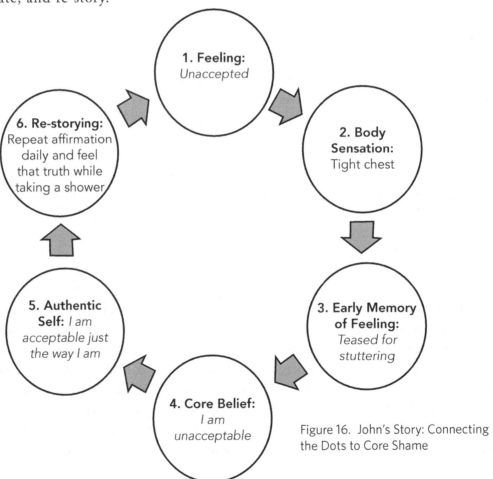

Figure 16. John's Story: Connecting the Dots to Core Shame

Ultimately, connecting the dots opens a doorway into a client's authentic truth. However, because the re-storying process is ongoing and nonlinear, clients are always working to re-story their authentic self. For example, John is continually re-storying and recognizes when the core shame belief of being unacceptable is triggered. For every client, feelings and connections will emerge in each session, which requires the therapist to attune with the client to be with what is surfacing and to help guide the connect-the-dots process. And then the process repeats, over and over again. Changing the sensory memory takes time and patience to stay with the process.

Connecting the dots may take one session, many sessions, or even months to years. Each part of the process leads to an uncovering of the core shame identity and has to be individualized for each client. Clinicians may simply stay with the feelings that emerged from the **Excavation Exercise** for a while, reflecting and validating the client's experience, while using large empathy. Most importantly, clinicians must pay attention to cues from the client about how far to go in each session, keeping in mind the client's window of tolerance and ensuring that therapy remains a place of safe emergency where the client is not asked to do too much, too fast.

Imagining a New Narrative

Although connecting the dots helps clients begin to write a new story, clients often can't identify how they feel or what they want. Since the client's core shame body memory often overrides any attempt to create a new narrative of a SAFE SELF, it is important to help clients understand that the new story is one that hasn't been written yet. Much like writing a novel, a blank page awaits, and the client needs to use their imagination to write something that has never been written before.

We can clearly see imagination in children, who play endless amounts of make-believe with scenes of schoolrooms, kitchens, hospitals, and so on. Reminding clients of this childlike wonder and inviting them to use imagination is an important part of shame-informed therapy for several reasons. First, it allows clients to activate the right brain and create new neural pathways, which is necessary for re-storying. **Imagining a new story of self-love and compassion through imagination and visualization provides the brain with the feeling of safety and begins the rewiring process.** Without visualizing something different, clients can only see what is familiar. Imagination expands possibility and hope. When unconscious material that clients have repressed comes to the surface in the imagination, they can use the material to re-story.

Second, using imagination allows clients to stretch into something new and different, which is important since writing a new narrative often feels foreign and unattainable. Clients initially might feel frustrated because they don't have a model for what they are re-storying. The cognitive story has been their truth for so long, which makes other options feel unattainable and out of the realm of possibility. By using the **Excavation Exercise** from chapter 2, clients have an opportunity to dig up what they feel and desire in specific situations. It stretches them to write about what they desire instead of what occurred—that is, to *imagine* the possibility of something new instead. Stretching into something new and different takes patience and a willingness to explore unfamiliar possibilities, and imagination expands possibility and hope as clients undergo this process.

Part of the process of tapping into imagination involves using the five senses so clients can imagine what they might touch, taste, see, hear, and smell in their new narrative. For example, if their new storyline is "I am lovable," they can think about what being lovable might feel, taste, look, sound, and smell like in their new story. It might *feel* like a tight hug, *taste* like their favorite childhood food, *look* like a friendly face, *sound* like a romantic love song, and *smell* like a bouquet of flowers. If clients can't recall any experiences associated with unconditional love, they can tap into the experience by picturing something or someone they love, thinking of spending time with a pet, remembering a time they felt appreciated, or thinking of a movie that portrays unconditional love. If possible, they can even find ways to actually engage each of their five senses as part of their re-story. If not, imagination works just fine!

Even with the use of imagination, though, it can still be challenging to help clients feel authenticity, joy, and safety in their body when the early wiring has been that of shame and fear. It takes time to override the old storylines, and the new story may feel uncomfortable at first. When this occurs, it can be helpful to draw on the adage often used in Alcoholics Anonymous, which teaches people in recovery to "fake it till you make it." Similarly, clients can act *as if* even when it doesn't feel quite natural. Like breaking in a new pair of stiff shoes, it will eventually feel more comfortable. Clinicians can then engage clients in the idea of writing a new safe story together, recognizing the paradoxical challenge and excitement of it never being written before.

In addition, clients frequently feel like they *should* be able to write a new story and get on with things quickly, as if it were a simple task. In turn, many clients feel shame when they struggle to develop a new narrative. To help normalize the client's experience, clinicians can provide psychoeducation and remind clients that the body memory always wins (van der Kolk, 2014). In particular, the body memory is so deeply engrained within the nervous system that any attempts to override it are often met with resistance. This neurobiology of shame makes the challenge of re-storying a common experience for *everyone*. This normalizes the client's experience and underscores the need for repetition and patience in the process. Even though clients may feel like they are lying to themselves when they repeat affirmations that they are lovable, it is actually the inborn truth of who they are, but the body memory has not allowed them access to that feeling prior to therapy.

Since the struggle to write a new narrative can evoke feelings of core shame, clinicians can also remind clients about the notion of transgenerational trauma, which explains why it is so hard to change old patterns embedded within our DNA. Moreover, clinicians can make clients aware of the twentieth-century research on social-emotional development that they might not know about. In having this discussion, a playful attitude can also be helpful. For example, in my own practice, I say, "We are the only species that has had to research itself to understand how to get along with each other. The animal kingdom does just fine." Providing a larger lens into this historical perspective, and explaining why it is so hard to change the old patterns embedded within our DNA, depersonalizes the experience of shame. When clients recognize that the challenge of change isn't just about them, but rather a more collective experience, that helps to minimize the core shame.

What Is a Functional Family?

To help illustrate the healthier attributes of a true SELF, clinicians may also find it useful to offer John Bradshaw's definition of a functional family (1988), as well as Virginia Satir's model of Five Freedoms (1983), both described here. These, and other resources you may have, can provide some storylines for the new narrative, which helps to take the edge off the struggle of writing something new that seems completely foreign and unfamiliar.

Drawing on Bradshaw's and Satir's work, you can use the letters in the word **FUNCTIONAL** as an acronym to give clients some new ideas as to how they may want to re-story their false narrative into a more authentic safe experience of living freely, or SELF:

- **F** refers to what Virginia Satir called the *Five Freedoms.* Satir spoke to the importance of being able to live freely with regard to the following five freedoms: (1) to see and hear what is, (2) to say what you feel and think, (3) to feel what you feel, (4) to ask for what you want, and (5) to take risks and be willing to rock the boat. This is in contrast to more typical dysfunctional family models based on outdated shame-based beliefs, such as "Do as I say, not as I do" and "You should be ashamed of yourself." Satir's model gives clients permission to be true to their SELF and to look at what that means for them in the new story.

- **U** represents the process through which intimacy *unfolds* in a marriage or partnership. In particular, there are several stages of intimacy that unfold in relationships, including falling in love, working through differences, compromising, individualizing, and achieving plateau intimacy. A healthy couple makes decisions based on an equal partnership, where each partner is responsible for their own individual lives. Some of the old family stories do not allow for this type of organic unfolding. Depending on what these narratives entail, various assumptions or expectations may arise. For instance, if someone believes that the feelings they experienced when they first fell in love should last forever, they may believe the relationship is over when conflict arises and they experience resentment and possibly even disgust. The unfolding of intimacy requires a willingness to move through all these feelings without the expectation that things will feel as they did in the beginning. The path of unfolding allows each individual to grow together through conflict, ideally creating a stronger bond.

- **N** is about *negotiating* differences, which is crucial to intimacy in relationships. To compromise, clients need to learn how to fight fair and to cooperate with others. However, this is challenging when working with core shame, as many of the defenses against shame may block a client's ability to negotiate differences.

- **C** stands for *clear and consistent communication.* Clients must be able to exhibit individual self-awareness to engage in clear communication. They must also have mutual respect for others so they can stay regulated and engage in productive and kind communication.

- **T** is all about *trust,* which is essential for emotional safety. When clients are able to honestly express their feelings and desires, this builds trust—even when this truth is not what other people want to hear. For example, reestablishing trust after an affair is usually difficult. It is necessary for clients to be honest going forward, even when it is hard, over a period of months or even years to rebuild trust.

- **I** encourages *individuality.* In a functional family, each member is allowed to make personal choices, and this individuality is made a priority. The old family paradigm often talked people out of their feelings and desires, but the new story allows for individuality.

- **O** relates to *openness* and flexibility. When clients are spontaneous without judgment or shame, this allows relationships to flow freely without too much rigidity. In their new story, being open to the ideas of others allows for more freedom and flow.
- **N** refers to getting one's emotional *needs* fulfilled. However, recognizing what one needs sometimes requires time and introspection. This isn't something that the client has done well in the old dysfunctional patterns, so it may take clients some time to recognize and honor their needs.
- **A** refers to taking *accountability* for behaviors. Functional families resolve problems by working together and taking ownership for each individual contribution to a situation. Similarly, part of the new narrative involves assuming responsibility for one's actions instead of resorting to defenses that involve blame or projection.
- **L** refers to the *laws* in a functional family, which are open and flexible in that they allow for mistakes and reparations. As clients work to rewrite their story, they, too, can give themselves permission to make mistakes—and then work on correcting those mistakes.

These ten descriptors of a FUNCTIONAL family can give clients an idea of what they want to have in the new narrative they are creating. Often, the challenge of writing a new story is not having an idea of what it is clients want. Bradshaw's model helps clients identify some goals and sets the stage for change.

Letter Writing

To help clients express their feelings and facilitate reintegration in the brain, it can be helpful to encourage them to write letters as part of the re-storying process. For example, clients may choose to write letters to loved ones who have passed on, especially if there is any complicated grief. Doing so can be therapeutic if there were things left unsaid or feelings that were unresolved. Anger is a stage of grief, and although it can seem inappropriate to be angry at someone for dying, giving clients the freedom to express whatever emotions emerge helps healing to occur.

Clients can also write letters that are not meant to be sent, as well as letters to and from their inner child. When clients write a letter with the knowledge that it will *not* be sent to the other person, this allows for freedom of expression, as well as an emotional release of any blocked energy in the body related to the situation. It allows clients to be completely honest and to let their feelings flow freely about topics that would otherwise be hurtful and nonproductive if actually said to the other person. After clients write this letter without worrying about what the other person will think, the therapist and client can then go back through the letter and highlight any main points that the client would like to possibly discuss with the person later on, or they may choose to use these points to draft an actual letter to the person that is more productive in nature.

Using Dreamwork and Fairy Tales to Re-Story

Dreams often offer up images that you can use in the re-storying process. Therefore, when a client brings a dream to a session, use it as an opportunity to gather information from the unconscious that can lead to healing core shame. There are many methods of dream analysis, but one popular framework is the projective model (Taylor, 1997). In this model, every dream image has an individual meaning for the dreamer, and dream dictionaries cannot universally speak directly to everyone's dream.

In projective work, the dreamer shares the dream with one or more people, and the persons hearing the dream respond with thoughts regarding what the dream may have meant. For instance, if someone has a dream about a horse, the clinician (or other group members) might share that a horse represents strength and power to them. They might also share some myth or fairy tale that mentions horses or any other reference to horses that has meaning to them. The clinician or group members would also ask the dreamer what a horse means to them. Through this process, the dreamer gains a sense of the various meanings behind the dream, and they can choose whatever interpretation is most helpful. It ultimately encourages the client to explore how aspects of the dream are parts of the self.

Working through dreams with another person or in a dream group can help the dreamer dig deeper into the unconscious and identify some hidden insights. When facilitating a dream group, there are a few important points that clinicians should keep in mind: (1) All dreams come in the service of health and wholeness, (2) Only the dreamer can say with any certainty what meanings their dream may have, (3) There is no such thing as a dream with only one meaning, (4) Dreams do not merely tell us what we already know, (5) Any remarks about a person's dream should be prefaced with something to the effect of "In my imagined version of the dream...", and (6) Anonymity must be maintained in all discussions. A handout at the end of this chapter provides more detailed guidelines for group dreamwork in accordance with Taylor's model.

Much like dreamwork, clinicians can draw on the use of fairy tales to facilitate the re-storying process. In Jungian psychology, every character in the story is viewed as an aspect of self, much like in dreamwork. By telling and listening to fairy tales, clients can turn on a switch to the collective unconscious and gain a deeper understanding of what the heart, mind, and soul feel. That is because archetypes are the backbone of fairy tales, mythology, and dreamwork—originating at the dawn of human history. These primordial images are everywhere and always present as expressions of human potential, needs, and instincts (Campbell, 1988). They relate to Carl Jung's idea of a collective unconscious, which is the commonality of the whole human race. Archetypes are universal symbols that activate the right brain, so when therapy evokes these archetypes, the right brain acknowledges something greater than oneself, creating a sense of connection and compassion for the story that can offer metaphors for healing.

There are numerous archetypes and ways to work with them for clients. If a client brings in a dream with a common archetype in it, or if something in waking life has an archetypal element, clinicians can work with the metaphors related to that archetype and how it is relevant to the client's personal re-story. Some common archetypes and their functions include the following: hero (service and sacrifice), mentor (guidance), threshold guardian (testing), herald (warning and challenge), shapeshifter (questioning and deception), shadow (destroying), and trickster (disrupting) (Voytilla, 1999). There are many books about archetypes that you can use for referencing some of the collective meanings. Two useful references are *Sacred Contracts* by Caroline Myss (2002) and *Awakening the Heroes Within* by Carol Pearson (1991).

We are neurobiologically wired for storytelling because it calls open the brain to perform multiple tasks simultaneously, such as sustaining attention, holding memory, tracking a sequence, recognizing emotions, and listening (Cozolino, 2002). Stories connect us to others and provide opportunities for self-reflection and moral lessons. In addition, combining the nonverbal emotion of a story with the linear storyline requires the use of both the right and left brain (Siegel, 1999).

Even though fairy tales are written for children, they offer stories that can heal inner-child memories by giving metaphors for transformation and redemption. Fairy tales have words and images that symbolize universal thought (Estés, 1995). To help clients re-story, you can ask them about a favorite fairy tale or story they remember from their childhood. If the story had a happy ending, invite them into the metaphor just as you would if you were working with a dream, and then see what they might want to create in their own life that will help them step into a metaphorical happy ending. If the story doesn't have a happy ending, ask the client to write a new ending and see how that might work out.

In the end, the goal is to simply help clients live a life that feels emotionally safe and free. Emotional safety is the goal, and the use of imagination, letter writing, dreamwork, and storytelling provides the framework to create those feelings in the body.

Exercises and Sample Re-Stories

The following exercises can help clients begin the process of re-storying their narrative into an authentic safe experience of living freely. The **My Freedom Manifesto** worksheet helps clients identify and name how they can live out the Five Freedoms in their life. The next two worksheets—**Letters To and From Me** and **Letter to Keep**—are good journal prompts for re-storying through letter writing.

The **Connect the Dots** worksheet asks clients to walk through the six steps of connecting the dots so they can write a new story and find ways to embody this new truth. **The Four R's** worksheet helps clients identify how they can move through the four R's with more consciousness whenever old shame beliefs become activated during the re-storying process. The **Come to Your Senses** worksheet provides suggestions for clients to imagine what the new story might be like using each of the five senses.

The **Dreamwork Toolkit** gives clinicians the tools they need to facilitate projective dreamwork safely and effectively, while the **Unfold Your Own Myth** worksheet assists clients in using their favorite fairy tales or mythology to inform the new story. To help clients brainstorm what they might want to include in this new story, they can also use the **Hindsight is 20/20** and **My Family's Screenplay** worksheets as a guide. These worksheets can give clients a better perspective on what it is they want and don't want in their new story.

Finally, **The Art and Architecture of Reconstructing the Authentic SELF: RE-STORYING** worksheet asks clients to finishing construction on their new "house" by adding art and decor that is more congruent with their true SELF.

My Freedom Manifesto

I, _____, declare that I will no longer see only what should be, was, or will be; say only what I think I should say; feel only what I was told I ought to feel; wait for permission to ask for what I want; and not take risks in order to *seem* secure. Instead, I commit to see and hear what is here, to say what I really feel and think, to feel what I feel, to ask for what I want, and to take risks on my behalf. I also commit to (add any others here):

_____

_____

_____

_____

Here are some ways I will step into my freedom manifesto:

_____

_____

_____

_____

_____

_____

Signed,

_____

Letters to and From Me

As you grow older and no longer depend on your parents, you may not remember your unmet childhood needs. Recognizing your inner child's unmet needs is the first step in repairing the ruptures in the interpersonal bridges to yourself. Writing a letter from your younger "little me" in your nondominant hand is a helpful tool to excavate those unmet needs. Let the memories and feelings flow onto the paper. Write whatever comes up until you feel finished.

A Letter from "Little Me"

Dear _____,

Signed,

Little _____

Now, have your "grown-up me" write back to your inner child in your dominant hand, assuring the child that you are always going to be there now, keeping things safe. You can use the space provided to write your letters, or you can use additional paper or your journal if you'd like.

A Letter from "Grown-Up Me"

Dear _____,

Signed,

Big _____

Letter to Keep

Sometimes, it can be helpful to write a letter to someone in your life to help you to identify what you are feeling. However, if you are overly direct and let your feelings flow freely, you may say things that are hurtful and nonproductive to the actual relationship. On the other hand, if you write a letter with the knowledge that you are *not* going to send it, it gives you the freedom to express your emotions without worrying about what the other person will think, which can help you release any pent-up energy you may be holding in your body.

You can use the space on the next page to write a letter to anyone who has stirred up some emotion in you in any way, either currently or in the past. After you write the letter, you can either keep it to yourself or go back and highlight any points you might want to discuss with the person at a later time. If so, you might choose to eventually write an actual letter to them. But this exercise is for you to freely express yourself, without any shame or judgment, knowing that this letter is for you to keep.

Letter to Keep

Today's Date:_____

Dear _____,

I am writing this letter to express what I am feeling about our relationship.

_____

_____

_____

_____

_____

_____

_____

_____

_____

_____

_____

_____

Sincerely,

_____

Connect the Dots

Identifying our feelings helps us connect to old core beliefs we learned as children. Since these beliefs live in unconscious body memories, we have to bring them into the light to change how we feel about ourselves. Re-storying these body memories involves giving the body cues of safety and trust. In this worksheet, you can begin to connect the dots and shift your old core shame beliefs so you can write a new story that involves a sense of safety.

1. **Feeling:** Name a feeling you are experiencing in a current situation in your life. The "Excavation Exercise" from chapter 2 is a useful tool to help you identify what you are feeling.

_____

_____

_____

_____

2. **Body Sensation:** Once you identify what you are feeling, check in with any bodily sensations that you might be having, such as a tight chest, a stiff neck, or nausea.

_____

_____

_____

_____

3. **Early Memory of Feeling:** If you are feeling too stressed to go on, take some deep breaths and take a little break for now. You can always come back to this later. If you are comfortable enough to keep going with the exercise, think back to an early memory when you experienced a similar feeling. Describe the event or memory. How old were you? What do you remember was happening?

_____

_____

_____

_____

4. Core Belief: Can you find a clue in the feeling you are describing that might have resulted in a core shame belief—one that you unconsciously developed as a truth about who you are? For example, if you felt unlovable when the event happened, then this may have resulted in a core shame belief that all of you is unlovable. Write that core shame belief here.

_____

_____

_____

_____

5. Authentic Self: Once you recognize your core shame belief, then you can begin to write a new story. Write what truly defines your authentic self. Don't worry if you don't believe it. Fake it until you make it! The truth of you is underneath the lies you have been told, and the body memory wants those lies to win. Keep telling your body the truth.

_____

_____

_____

_____

6. Re-Story: Now, think of things you enjoy doing and commit to bringing your authentic self into those experiences. Breathe into the authentic self. Feel the feelings of the old core shame wash away like sand on the shore. Re-story the truth of who you are by feeling body sensations of love, worthiness, joy, and belonging.

_____

_____

_____

_____

The Four R's

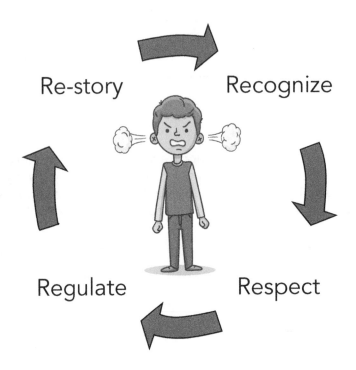

Re-story   Recognize

Regulate   Respect

Most of the time, when we are in an emotionally charged situation, it is hard to think clearly and act rationally. Old shame beliefs can get activated, and our capacity to act maturely and respond with clarity goes out the window! Renowned scientist Stephen Porges has developed the polyvagal theory to explain what happens in the autonomic nervous system during these times of stress. When we *recognize* this autonomic reaction to stress and *respect* that it has helped us to cope through the years, we then can learn to *regulate* our emotions and *re-story* a sense of safety in the body, which eventually helps us respond more effectively in difficult situations. The next time you are feeling emotionally charged and unable to think clearly, take a deep breath and ask yourself the following:

RECOGNIZE: What is my behavior here? Am I responding by lashing out, avoiding, being passive-aggressive, overcompensating and doing too much, or in some other way? What am I feeling? Make notes here about whatever answers emerge from these questions:

_____

_____

_____

_____

_____

_____

_____

RESPECT: Whatever behaviors you *recognized* previously are reactions that you developed over time for the sake of safety and survival. When you were a young child, you created a story that helped you feel safe, which may have involved being defiant, lashing out, avoiding, or people pleasing. How can you respect how these choices helped you cope? Make some notes here about how your reaction in this situation has seemed to help you feel safe through the years. For example, perhaps you told yourself, "If I avoid this situation and isolate myself, then I won't have to face criticism and shame," or "If I defend myself and argue with you, then you will eventually understand and love me."

_____

_____

_____

_____

_____

REGULATE: Now that you *recognize* and *respect* your reaction, you can begin to regulate your emotions by taking a deep breath and coming into present-moment mindfulness. Realizing that the old coping patterns were just an illusion of safety and not necessarily the best choices, you can begin to find safety in the breath and the present moment without having to react to the situation. Simply be present. Pay attention to your body sensations. Use this space to make a note of where you may be feeling any tension in your body. Then, breathe self-compassion into that area and describe the experience of doing that. Is there resistance, doubt, calm, or something else? What does it feel like?

_____

_____

_____

_____

_____

_____

_____

RESTORY: Once you begin to *recognize, respect,* and *regulate* your reactions, you are bringing what has been unconscious to consciousness. Once you become more conscious of these coping patterns, you can begin to choose some new patterns instead. Think of what you would prefer in this situation and imagine what it might be like to respond differently next time. Perhaps you can use one or more of the 4 "C" shovels: courage, curiosity, compassion, and connection. What would be different if you choose one of these reactions instead of resorting to your typical reaction? Write a new story here:

_____

_____

_____

_____

_____

_____

_____

Come to Your Senses

When re-storying a new narrative of a SAFE SELF, it can be difficult to imagine what the new story might feel like in your body, especially if you don't have any model or template to go by. For example, perhaps you are working on the new storyline "I am lovable" but have found it difficult to embody this affirmation because it is unfamiliar. To help you imagine the experience of being lovable, you can tap into your five senses to imagine what being lovable might look, sound, smell, taste, and feel like. For example, perhaps "I am lovable" *looks* like a welcoming smile, *sounds* like the song "I Am Only Love," *smells* like roses, *tastes* like mashed potatoes, and *feels* like a soft warm blanket. To help you brainstorm, you can even think of times when you may have felt lovable or seen others exhibit unconditional love, maybe in a movie or book. Then, if possible, find ways to actually embody this affirmation through sight, sound, touch, taste, or smell. If not, imagination works just fine!

My affirmation is:

_____

_____

If I were to embody my affirmation, it might:

Look like _____

Sound like _____

Smell like _____

Taste like _____

Feel like _____

The Dreamwork Toolkit

1. All dreams speak a universal language of metaphor and symbols, and they come in the service of health and wholeness. There is no such thing as a "bad" dream—only dreams that sometimes take a dramatically negative form to grab our attention.

2. Only the dreamer can say with any certainty what meanings the dream may have. This certainty usually comes in the form of a wordless *aha* of recognition. This aha moment is a function of memory and is the only reliable touchstone of dreamwork.

3. There is no such thing as a dream with only one meaning. All dreams and dream images are overdetermined in that they have multiple meanings and layers of significance.

4. Dreams do not just come to tell you what you already know. All dreams break new ground and invite you to new understandings and insights.

5. When talking to others about their dreams, it is both wise and polite to preface your remarks with words to the effect of "In my imagined version of the dream..." and to keep this commentary in the first person as much as possible. This means you should frame even relatively challenging comments in such a way that the dreamer may hear and internalize them. It also can become a profound psychospiritual discipline of "walking a mile in your neighbor's moccasins."

6. All dream-group participants should agree at the outset to maintain anonymity in all discussions of dreamwork. In the absence of any specific request for confidentiality, group members should be free to discuss their experiences openly outside the group, provided no other dreamer is identifiable in their stories. However, whenever any group member requests confidentiality, all members should agree to be bound automatically by such a request.

Source: From *The Wisdom of Your Dreams* by Jeremy Taylor, Penguin Books, 2009.
Unlimited distribution with proper attribution is encouraged.

Unfold Your Own Myth

Think about a favorite fairy tale or story that you remember from childhood. If the story had a happy ending, imagine what you might want to create in your life that will help you step into the metaphorical happy ending. If the story doesn't have a happy ending, write a new ending and see how that metaphor might work out. This worksheet gives you some questions to think about as you rewrite your new story.

1. What was your favorite story or fairy tale as a child?

_____

_____

_____

2. What was it about the story that you connected with?

_____

_____

_____

3. How does the story relate to your life now?

_____

_____

_____

4. If it had a happy ending, imagine the path you could take to create your own life story that way.

_____

_____

_____

5. If the story did not have a happy ending, what can you do to rewrite the story for yourself? (Keep in mind health and wholeness as the goal. Be sure to include self-love and compassion.)

_____

_____

_____

"Don't be satisfied with stories, how things have gone for others. Unfold your own myth."
—Rumi

Hindsight is 20/20

Sometimes, it is hard to know what we want to create for ourselves. We seem to know what we *don't* want, but identifying something new and improved that we *do* want can be difficult. They say that hindsight is 20/20, so thinking about what you don't want may help you write a new story. Think of it as a brand-new novel that has never been written.

In the left-hand column, make a list of all the things you don't really like in your life—things that deplete your energy, make you feel frustrated or irritated, or just don't feel aligned with who you want to be. Then, in the right-hand column, think of what it is you desire that corresponds with the opposite of what you wrote in the left-hand column. Finally, on the next page, fill in the image of your new SELF with these desired aspects of your life, and write down or draw images of what those things might feel like in your body.

The Things in My Life I *Don't* Like	The Things I *Do* Want
Example: Arguments with my partner	Example: Conflict resolution and better communication

Here is your new strong SELF! Write or draw all the imagined things you want. Then, close your eyes and imagine what those things might feel like in your body. For example, if you want conflict resolution and better communication, perhaps this is associated with feeling *light as a feather*. Or if you want more time to paint, perhaps this is associated with a feeling of *relaxation*.

My Family's Screenplay

Oftentimes, when you start doing inner work in therapy and uncovering old patterns, visiting with your family can be triggering. The next time you are with your family, imagine that you are watching them in a movie—a movie that you are simply observing but not a part of. Step out of the movie and observe what is happening without getting tangled in all the emotions that might typically arise. Doing so will help you get a better perspective regarding your family's dynamics so you can see what it is you want and don't want in your new story.

Use this worksheet to give the movie a title, name the conflict or problem, and imagine what might be a solution to the problem. Remember, you are witnessing your family as a way to see what you want to change and do differently. You are not emotionally attached.

Movie Title: _____

Main Conflict or Problem: _____

_____

_____

Possible Solution: _____

_____

Reconstructing the Authentic Self
RE-STORYING a New Narrative
(Art and Decor)

Give yourself permission to think about the things that make your house a home and also what makes your life congruent with your desires. Using this house as a guide, you can think of re-storying as the process of adding art and decor to your newly designed house that is updated and more congruent with your true SELF.

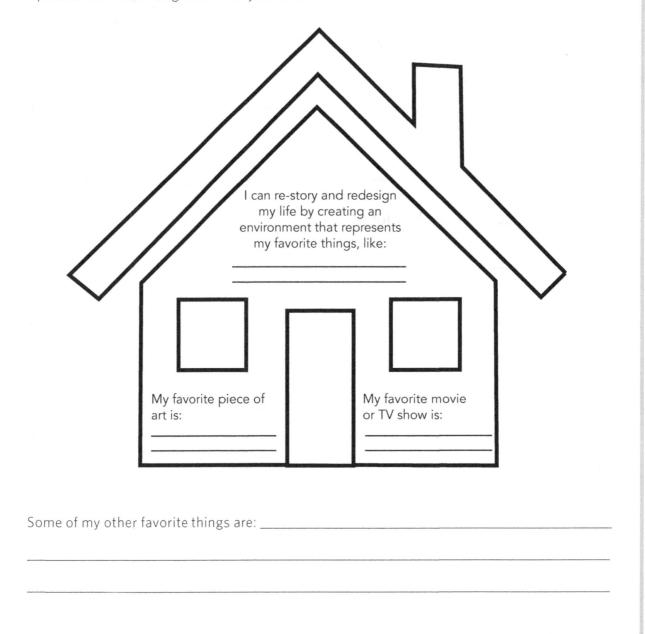

I can re-story and redesign my life by creating an environment that represents my favorite things, like:
_____
_____

My favorite piece of art is:
_____
_____

My favorite movie or TV show is:
_____
_____

Some of my other favorite things are: _____
_____
_____

Sample Re-Story: An Inconvenience (Jennifer)

Jennifer was a thirty-five-year-old mother who came to therapy because of minor conflicts with her husband and children. When she and her husband moved to Colorado, her mother told her it was inconvenient for her. The word *inconvenient* continued to emerge in our therapy sessions, suggesting that her core shame identity involved viewing herself as an inconvenience. Her parenting style also reflected some of the ways her father had parented. He was demanding and had high expectations. Jennifer commented that her son liked to "smell the flowers," and she especially got frustrated with his laid-back and slow behavior. One of her homework assignments was to write a letter in her nondominant hand from her inner child about her memories surrounding her father's demanding and punitive discipline. Then, she wrote a letter back to her inner child in her dominant hand, reassuring her inner child that she was lovable and not an inconvenience.

Although Jennifer said the exercise felt awkward and uncomfortable, she realized that she felt sad about what happened to her as a child. It also helped her to have more empathy for her son and his behavior.

Old Story: I am an inconvenience.

Re-Story: I am lovable as I am.

Sample Re-Story: It's Okay to Be Me (Stuart)

Stuart was a twenty-four-year-old with attention-deficit/hyperactivity disorder (ADHD) who had been struggling with his manager at work. He felt like he was not getting clear instructions or guidance in terms of his daily job expectations. Recently, he also experienced a nightmare about his middle-school teacher from childhood. As a child, he had been afraid of being called on in class, worried that he would be embarrassed and humiliated for not knowing the correct answer. The dream he had was much like what had happened when he was a young boy. He woke up humiliated and even more anxious about getting it right at work. Looking at the dream as it appeared in his earlier life was as far as he could go with the meaning, which then led to the familiar feeling of humiliation and defeat. I asked him what his little boy needed. His response was, "I need to be more focused and pay attention." I told him that is what the boy thought at the time, which led to his feelings of not being good enough.

The truth is that the little boy needed the teacher to understand how he was feeling anxious and scared in class. I suggested he imagine going back into the dream and telling the teacher what he needed at the time.

Old Story: To be successful in school or work, I need to be more focused and pay attention.

Re-Story: I recognize that my ADHD gives me a different learning style. It is okay to be me and ask for help.

9

The Hero's Journey

"Darth Vader has not developed his own humanity. He's a robot. He's a bureaucrat, living not in terms of himself but in terms of an imposed system. This is the threat to our lives that we all face today. Is the system going to flatten you out and deny your humanity, or are you going to be able to make use of the system to the attainment of human purposes?"

—Joseph Campbell

Excavating the Authentic SELF

Reconstructing a new story is not an easy task. There isn't a smooth path from start to finish. Embracing paradox, facing one's fears, meeting the unconscious, and coming back into wholeness are all parts of the deep work of healing shame and finding the authentic self. This work requires willingness and tenacity to stay with the process.

Joseph Campbell called this quest for inner wholeness a hero's journey (1990, 2008). It represents a twelve-step circular journey where one encounters the unconscious to integrate parts of the self and move in the direction of wholeness (Figure 17). Across these twelve steps, there are four major stages that outline the process of personal transformation: the call, the quest, the reward, and the return. On the journey, one is asked to leave behind the false self in search of the authentic truth that lies hidden deep inside. It is an inner expedition of self-discovery, excavating the truth that lies within. As we see in stories, there is never an easy path. Everyone has to face obstacles in life and overcome them in ways that allow for a safe experience of living freely. This chapter will examine how the hero's journey is relevant to working with shame and reconstructing the authentic SELF.

The Shame-Informed Hero's Journey

The Call

The moral objective in the hero's journey lies in saving something. In the case of shame-informed therapy, it is about saving the true SELF. The hero's journey starts in the *ordinary world,* where one is oblivious of the adventures to come. Then, something happens that threatens or questions safety and disrupts the ordinary world, and it ignites the *call to adventure.*

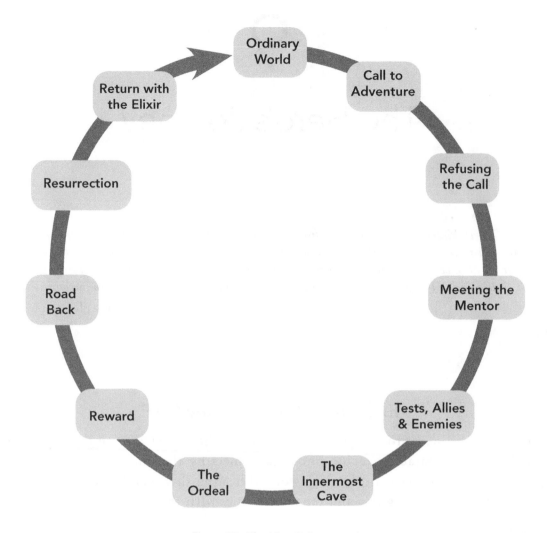

Figure 17. The Hero's Journey

Something may have happened that feels unsettling or uncomfortable, such as death, divorce, illness, addiction, or any other life event where something feels lacking or lost.

At first, one typically *refuses the call*, fearing a presumed threat. Self-doubt leads to a refusal to listen as it seems too much to handle. Eventually, the call is followed and one sets out on the journey of finding the true SELF. This cycle can happen repeatedly throughout life, as different situations occur that evoke suffering.

Answering the call then leads to *meeting the mentor*. Often, this is a therapist or coach who provides guidance. The mentor helps dispel the doubts and fears and provides strength and courage to begin the quest. When a client decides to seek therapy, it is usually after hearing and possibly refusing the call to adventure.

The Quest

Once ready to begin the quest, the hero willingly, or sometimes reluctantly, crosses the threshold between the familiar and unfamiliar worlds. The hero then meets *tests, allies,* and *enemies.*

The hero is out of their comfort zone and is now confronted with obstacles or people trying to thwart the progress. The hero needs to learn whom to trust. Allies and enemies prepare the hero for greater ordeals to come. Every obstacle helps gain a deeper insight into the hero's personal identity. In relation to the therapeutic relationship, this is the foundation of the work, where the clinician establishes trust and safety as the client faces fears and challenges.

Next is the *approach to the inmost cave,* which represents terrible danger or inner conflict. The hero must prepare to leap into the unknown. At the threshold to the cave, the hero once again faces doubts and fears. The hero needs time to reflect on the journey and the treacherous road ahead to find courage to continue. This brief respite helps the hero understand the magnitude of the ordeal, escalating the anticipation of the ultimate test. This can relate to the time in therapy when a client feels they can face the deeper core shame and look at what they have hidden for so long.

Then comes *the ordeal.* This might be an inner crisis that requires the hero to face deep fear. The hero must draw on the skills that they have gathered on the path to overcome this most difficult challenge. After overcoming the greatest challenge, the hero is ultimately transformed and stronger. This is why therapy takes times. Facing one's fears and shame from the past requires tenacity and willingness to stay on the journey.

The Reward

Overcoming the greatest challenge is *the reward,* which may come in the form of an object, a secret, greater knowledge or insight, or even reconciliation with a loved one. Whatever the reward, the hero must now prepare for the last leg of the journey, *the road back.* This stage represents a return home with the reward. But it isn't over yet. The hero may have to choose between a personal objective and a higher cause. This is the time in therapy when the client starts to realize that the internal battles were ultimately worth it. The true self starts to feel more congruent, and life seems to make more sense.

The final battle is the *resurrection.* This represents something greater than the hero's own existence and has far-reaching consequences to the ordinary world. This might occur when the client realizes that the familiar confabulations they came to know were a part of a larger collective story and that they were never really on their own.

The Return

The final stage is *the return with the elixir*, where the hero comes back to the ordinary world completely transformed. But things will never be the same. Clients may try to explain their journey to family and friends and discover they don't understand, nor do they really care. This is when a client deepens the awareness of their own individuation and can celebrate the SELF, knowing they have found their authentic self and no longer need validation from others.

Using the hero's journey as a model for transformation helps clients understand that life involves struggle and that writing a story more aligned with the authentic self often comes only after a complex quest for wholeness.

Exercises

On the pages that follow, clients will have an opportunity to reflect on their own therapeutic journey by using **The Hero's Journey** worksheet. It is best to use this worksheet toward the end of therapy so clients can review the work they have done. As with all the worksheets, use discretion in the timing and presentation of this exercise so as not to evoke more shame. Although this worksheet provides a useful roadmap of the client's journey, it may feel overwhelming if given too soon. Clinicians can also use this worksheet as a reference to see where a client may be at certain points in therapy without actually giving it to the client.

The Hero's Journey

Reconstructing a new story of an authentic self is similar to what Joseph Campbell called a hero's journey. This journey involves four major stages—the call, the quest, the reward, and the return—and there isn't a smooth, easy path from start to finish. Writing a new story for yourself that is more congruent with who you really are requires facing ordeals much like in mythology and stories. Use this worksheet to write about your hero's journey as you see it today. Which stage are you currently in? Write about each one as you feel it is relevant to your inner work.

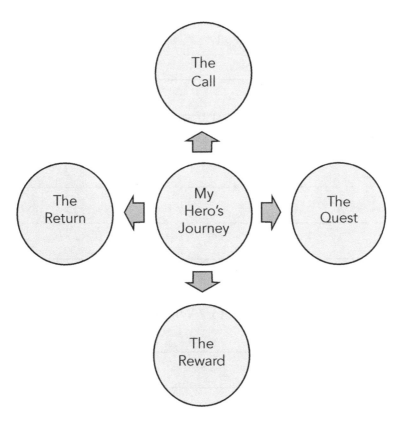

The Call: Here, in the *ordinary world*, something happens that threatens your safety and you are *called to adventure*. Death, divorce, illness, addiction, or other difficult life events initiate the call. At first, you may *refuse the call* because if seems too hard. But eventually you follow it and *meet your mentor*. A therapist, coach, or other teacher provides guidance and courage to begin the quest.

Write about when you heard **the call** here. Include what happened that encouraged you to step out of the ordinary world, what resistance you may have had, who it was that helped you find your mentor, and who is (or was) your mentor.

1. What happened that encouraged you to step out of the ordinary world and follow the call?

_____

_____

_____

_____

_____

2. What resistance did you have to the call?

_____

_____

_____

_____

_____

3. Who or what helped you find your mentor? Who is (or was) your mentor?

_____

_____

_____

_____

_____

4. What else do you want to say about the call?

_____

_____

_____

_____

_____

_____

The Quest: Now you cross the threshold between the familiar and unfamiliar, encountering *tests, allies, and enemies*. You begin to discern whom it is you can trust. Every obstacle helps you gain insight into your identity. Then, you leap into the unknown, *the inmost cave*, where you face inner conflict, doubts, and fears. As you reflect on the journey, you somehow find the courage to continue. Next is *the ordeal,* which requires you to face even deeper fear. After you overcome this challenging quest, you are transformed and stronger. This is why therapy takes time. Facing deep core shame and what has been hidden from the past requires tenacity and a willingness to stay on the journey.

Write about your **quest** here. Include what you are recognizing in therapy about your deeper fears and doubts; who and what are your tests, allies, and enemies; what helps you stay on the journey; and what insights you are gaining regarding your true identity.

1. What you are recognizing about your deeper fears and doubts?

_____

_____

_____

_____

_____

_____

2. Who and what are your tests, allies, and enemies?

_____

_____

_____

_____

_____

_____

3. What helps you stay on the journey?

_____

_____

_____

_____

_____

_____

4. What insights are you gaining regarding your true identity?

_____

_____

_____

_____

_____

_____

5. What else do you want to say about your quest?

_____

_____

_____

_____

_____

_____

The Reward: Having had the willingness and tenacity to stay on the journey, you have now earned your *reward*. This reward may be an object, knowledge, insight, or even reconciliation with a loved one. As you prepare to take *the road back* with your reward, you may have to choose between a personal objective and a higher cause. Your authentic SELF feels more congruent, and you strive to take your hard-earned reward and wisdom back to the ordinary world. Finally, there is a *resurrection* as you integrate something greater than your existence into the ordinary world. You realize how the family stories and confabulations were never really your own.

Write about **the reward** here. Include any insights, secrets, greater knowledge, or reconciliations that occurred; how you prepared for the road back to the ordinary world; what choices you made between personal objectives and a higher cause; and what you now recognize about your family story that is not congruent with who you really are.

1. What insights, secrets, greater knowledge, or reconciliations occurred?

_____

_____

_____

_____

_____

_____

2. How did you prepare for the road back to the ordinary world?

_____

_____

_____

_____

_____

3. What choices did you have to make between personal objectives and a higher cause?

_____

_____

_____

_____

_____

4. What do you now recognize about your family story that is not congruent with who you really are?

_____

_____

_____

_____

_____

5. What else do you want to say about the reward?

_____

_____

_____

_____

_____

_____

The Return: *Returning with the elixir,* you come back to the ordinary world completely transformed, and nothing will ever be the same. Trying to explain your journey to family and friends is fruitless because they will never truly understand. Your deeper self-awareness leads you to a celebration as you now can live out a safe experience of living freely. You no longer need validation from others. You are more aligned with your authentic self after your hero's journey.

Write about **the return** here. Describe what things will never be the same, what happened when you tried to explain the journey to your friends and family, and what it feels like to be more aligned with your authentic self.

1. What things feel like they will never be the same?

_____

_____

_____

_____

_____

2. What happened when you tried to explain the journey to your friends and family?

_____

_____

_____

_____

_____

_____

3. What does it feel like to be more aligned with your authentic self?

_____

_____

_____

_____

_____

_____

4. What else do you want to say about the return?

_____

_____

_____

_____

_____

_____

Conclusion

"Be patient toward all that is unsolved in your heart and try to love the questions themselves, like locked rooms and like books that are now written in a very foreign tongue. Do not now seek the answers, which cannot be given you because you would not be able to live them. And the point is, to live everything. Live the questions now. Perhaps you will then gradually, without noticing it, live along some distant day into the answer."

—Rainer Maria Rilke

Helping clients heal core shame takes patience and tenacity to stay with the process. It took a while for the shame to get wired into the mind and body, and it also takes time to change those neural connections. Just like clients can use the four "C" shovels to override the shame response, clinicians can use the four "C" shovels in their therapeutic work: by exhibiting *curiosity* and leading with questions instead of trying to move too quickly to solutions, by having the *courage* to tolerate dysregulated emotional states and projections, by showing *compassion* to meet clients where they are, and by drawing on *connection* to repair any ruptured interpersonal bridges.

Clients may get frustrated with what can sometimes seem like an endless process. This can then trigger shame. It is not unusual to experience a breakthrough one week and then have the shame reemerge the following week. Once therapists recognize core shame and the defenses against it, therapeutic outcomes tend to change. The unconscious becomes more conscious over time, and clients begin to feel more emotionally safe in their bodies. Always keep in mind the goal of a safe experience of living freely, or SELF, and what that means as the client moves through the four therapeutic R's.

In addition, exhibiting self-awareness and engaging in self-care are so important for clinicians. Working with right-brain co-regulation requires a lot of emotional, physical, and mental stamina. When mirror neurons are activated while processing a client's shame, we feel shame with them, and this can be draining. Therefore, make sure to take the time to care for yourself. You can use the following self-care love note to help you (or your clients) find love and compassion during this process. Healing shame takes time. Have compassion for yourself in the process. Namasté.

A Love Note to SELF

Date: _____

Dear_____,

Remember to:

1. _____

2. _____

3. _____

4. _____

5. _____

Love,

_____

Put this on your bulletin board or refrigerator to remind
yourself to take care of YOU!

Bibliography

For your convenience, you may download a pdf version of the worksheets
in this book from our dedicated website: **pesi.com/Ashley**

Akhtar, S. (2009). *Comprehensive dictionary of psychoanalysis.* New York: Routledge.

Albom, M. (1997). *Tuesdays with Morrie: An old man, a young man, and life's greatest lesson.* New York: Doubleday.

Andrews, T. (2002). *Animal speak: The spiritual & magical powers of creatures great & small.* St. Paul, MN: Llewellyn Worldwide.

Angelou, M. (2009). *I know why the caged bird sings.* New York: Random House.

Bolen, J. S. (1994). *Crossing to Avalon: A woman's midlife pilgrimage.* San Francisco, CA: Harpercollins.

Bradshaw, J. (1988). *Bradshaw on: The family.* Deerfield Beach, FL: Health Communications.

Brown, B. (2007). *I thought it was just me (but it isn't): Making the journey from "What will people think?" to "I am enough."* New York: Avery.

Brown, B. (2010a). *The gifts of imperfection: Let go of who you think you're supposed to be and embrace who you are.* Center City, MN: Hazelden.

Brown, S. (2010b). *Play: How it shapes the brain, opens the imagination, and invigorates the soul.* New York: Penguin.

Brown, J. Huntley, D., Morgan, S., Dodson, K. D., & Cich, J. (2017). Confabulation: A guide for mental health professionals. *International Journal of Neurology and Neuropathy, 4*(2), 1–9. https://doi.org/10.23937/2378-3001/1410070

Campbell, J. (1988). *The power of myth.* New York: Doubleday.

Campbell, J. (1990). *The hero's journey: Joseph Campbell on his life and work* (P. Cousineau, Ed.). New York: Harper & Row.

Campbell, J. (2008). *The hero with a thousand faces* (3rd ed.). Novato, CA: New World Library.

Campion, M., & Glover, L. (2017). A qualitative exploration of responses to self-compassion in a non-clinical sample. *Health Social Care Community, 25*(3), 1100–1108. https://doi.org/10.1111/hsc.12408

Childre, D., & Martin, H. (2000). *The HeartMath solution.* New York: Harpercollins.

Cozolino, L. (2002). *The neuroscience of psychotherapy: Building and rebuilding the human brain.* New York: W. W. Norton.

Cozolino, L. (2010). *The neuroscience of psychotherapy: Healing the social brain* (2nd ed.). New York: W. W. Norton.

Dana, D. (2018). *The polyvagal theory in therapy: Engaging the rhythm of regulation.* New York: W. W. Norton.

DeYoung, P. A. (2015). *Understanding and treating chronic shame: A relational/neurobiological approach.* New York: Routledge.

Erikson, E. H. (1968). *Identity: Youth and crisis.* New York: W. W. Norton.

Estés, C. P. (1995). *Women who run with the wolves: Myths and stories of the wild woman archetype.* New York: Random House.

Fincher, S. F. (1991). *Creating mandalas: For insight, healing, and self-expression.* Boston, MA: Shambhala.

Gawain, S. (2002). *Creative visualization: Use the power of your imagination to create what you want in your life.* Navato, CA: New World Library.

Gundel, F., von Spee, J., Schneider, S., Haeussinger, F. B., Hautzinger, M., Erb, M., ... Ehlis, A. C. (2018). Meditation and the brain: Neuronal correlates of mindfulness assessed with near-infrared spectroscopy. *Psychiatry Research: Neuroimaging, 271,* 24–33.

Hendricks, G., & Hendricks, K. (2016). *Conscious loving ever after: How to create thriving relationships at midlife and beyond.* New York: Hay House.

Herman, J. L. (2007). *Shattered shame states and their repair.* From the John Bowlby Memorial Lecture. March 10, 2007. Department of Psychiatry, Harvard Medical School.

Heussenstamm, P. (2016). *Mandalas: A coloring book.* Portland, OR: Pomegranate Communications.

Jordan, J. V. (1997). Relational development through mutual empathy. In A. C. Bohart & L. S. Greenberg (Eds.), *Empathy reconsidered: New directions in psychotherapy* (pp. 343–351). Washington, DC: American Psychological Association.

Jung, C. G. (1963). *Memories, dreams, reflections* (A. Jaffe, Ed., R. Winston & C. Winston, Trans.). New York: Random House.

Kabat-Zinn, J. (2005). *Coming to our senses: Healing ourselves and the world through mindfulness.* New York: Hyperion.

Kaufman, G. (1974, August). *On shame, identity and the dynamics of change.* Paper presented at the 82nd meeting of the American Psychological Association, New Orleans, LA.

Kaufman, G. (1992). *Shame: The power of caring* (3rd ed.). Rochester, VT: Schenkman Books.

Keng, S., & Tan, J. X. (2017). Effects of brief mindful breathing and loving-kindness meditation on shame and social problem-solving abilities among individuals with borderline personality traits. *Behavior Research and Therapy, 97,* 43–51. https://doi.org/10.1016/j.brat.2017.07.004

Kersey, K. (1983). *The art of sensitive parenting: Ten keys to raising confident, competent, and responsible children.* New York: Berkley Books.

Kohut, J. (1984). *How does analysis cure?* Chicago: University of Chicago Press.

Knox, J. (2013). "Feeling for" and "feeling with": Developmental and neuroscientific perspectives on intersubjectivity and empathy. *The Journal of Analytic Psychology, 58,* 491–509.

Levine, P. (2010). *In an unspoken voice: How the body releases trauma and restores goodness.* Berkley, CA: North Atlantic Books.

Lewis, H. B. (1971). *Shame and guilt in neurosis.* New York: International University Press.

Lewis, H. B. (1988). The role of shame in symptom formation. In M. Clynes & J. Panksepp (Eds.), *Emotions and psychopathology* (pp. 95–106). Boston, MA: Springer.

Lipton, B. (2005). *The biology of belief: Unleashing the power of consciousness, matter & miracles.* New York: Hay House.

Miller, A. (1983). *For your own good: Hidden cruelty in child-rearing and the roots of violence.* New York: Noonday Press.

Myss, C. (2002). *Sacred contracts.* New York: Three Rivers Press.

Neff, K. (2003). Self-compassion: An alternative conceptualization of a healthy attitude toward oneself. *Self and Identify, 2*(2), 85–101. https://doi.org/10.1080/15298860309032

Ogden, P. (2003). *Building somatic resources* (Unpublished doctoral dissertation). Union Institute and University, Cincinnati, OH.

Oliver, M. (1992). *House of light.* Boston, MA: Beacon Press.

Pearson, C. (1991). *Awakening the heroes within.* New York: Harpercollins.

Piaget, J. (1969). *The psychology of the child.* New York: Basic Books.

Porges, S. W. (2004). Neuroception: A subconscious system for detecting threats and safety. *Zero to Three, 24*(5), 19–24.

Porges, S. W. (2009). The polyvagal theory: New insights into adaptive reactions of the autonomic nervous system. *Cleveland Clinic Journal of Medicine, 76*(Suppl 2), S86–S90. https://doi.org/10.3949/ccjm.76.s2.17

Porges, S. W. (2011). *The polyvagal theory: Neurophysiological foundations of emotions, attachment, communication, self-regulation.* New York: W. W. Norton.

Porges, S. W. (2017). *The pocket guide to the polyvagal theory: The transformative power of feeling safe.* New York: W. W. Norton.

Retzinger, S. M. (1995). Identifying shame and anger in discourse. *American Behavioral Scientist, 38*(8), 1104–1113. https://doi.org/10.1177/0002764295038008006

Rilke, M. R. (1993). *Letters to a young poet.* New York: W. W. Norton.

Rogers, C. R. (1957). The necessary and sufficient conditions of therapeutic personality change. *Journal of Consulting Psychology, 21*(2), 95–103. https://doi.org/10.1037/h0045357

Rogers, C. R. (1961). *On becoming a person: A therapist's view of psychotherapy.* Boston, MA: Houghton Mifflin.

Rosas, D., & Rosas, C. (2005). *The Nia technique: The high-powered energizing workout that gives you a new body and a new life.* New York: Broadway Books.

Rosenberg, S. (2017). *Accessing the healing power of the vagus nerve.* Berkley, CA: North Atlantic Books.

Rothschild, B. (2000). *The body remembers: The psychophysiology of trauma and trauma treatment.* New York: W. W. Norton.

Satir, V. (1983). *Conjoint family therapy.* Palo Alto, CA: Science and Behavior Books.

Schore, A. N. (2012). *The science of the art of psychotherapy.* New York: W. W. Norton.

Schore, A. N. (2014). Early interpersonal neurobiological assessment of attachment and autistic spectrum disorders. *Frontiers in Psychology, 5,* 1049. https://doi.org/10.3389/fpsyg.2014.01049

Schore, A. N. (2019). *Right brain psychotherapy.* New York: W. W. Norton.

Siegel, D. J. (1999). *The developing mind: Toward a neurobiology of interpersonal experience.* New York: Guilford Press.

Siegel, D. J. (2007). *The mindful brain: Reflection and attunement in the cultivation of well-being.* New York: W. W. Norton.

Siegel, D. J. (2010). *Mindsight: The new science of personal transformation.* New York: Bantam Books.

Taylor, J. (2009). *The wisdom of your dreams.* New York: Penguin Books.

Youssef, N. A., Lockwood, L., Su, S., Hao, G., & Rutten, B. P. (2018). The effects of trauma, with or without PTSD, on transgenerational DNA methylation alterations in human offsprings. *Brain Science, 8*(5), 83. https://doi.org/10.3390/brainsci8050083

van der Kolk, B. (2014). *The body keeps the score: Brain, mind, and body in the healing of trauma.* New York: Penguin Books.

Voytilla, S. (1999). *Myth and the movies.* Studio City, CA: Michael Wiese Productions.

Whitfield, C. L. (1987). *Healing the child within: Discovery and recovery for adult children of dysfunctional families.* Deerfield Beach, FL: Health Communications.

Willard, C., Abblett, M., & Desmond, T. (2016). *The self-compassion deck: 50 mindfulness-based practices.* Eau Claire, WI: PESI Publishing & Media.

Willis, K., & Lee, P. J. (1990). *Tales from the night rainbow.* Honolulu, HI: Night Rainbow Publishing.

Winnicott, D. W. (1986). *Home is where we start from: Essays by a psychoanalyst.* New York: W. W. Norton.

Wiseman, T. (1996). A concept analysis of empathy. *Journal of Advanced Nursing, 23*(6), 1162–1167. https://doi.org/10.1046/j.1365-2648.1996.12213.x.

Woods, H., & Proeve, M. (2014). Relationships of mindfulness, self-compassion, and meditation experience with shame-proneness. *Journal of Cognitive Psychotherapy, 28,* 20–23. https://doi.org/10.1891/0889-8391.28.1.20

Yard, M. A. (2014). The changing faces of shame: Theoretical underpinnings and clinical management. *Issues in Psychoanalytic Psychology, 36,* 42–54.

Made in the USA
Middletown, DE
21 October 2023